Loving Lisa

Stolen Life, Stolen Dreams

Loving Lisa

Stolen Life, Stolen Dreams

ANGELA DOYLE-STUART

HMD PUBLISHING

Published by Hayes MacDermot Publishing
Unit 11, Tandy's Lane
Lucan, Co Dublin
Ireland
www.irishbooksandauthors.com

First published, 2012

A CIP record for this book is available from the British Library

ISBN 978-0-9574482-0-9

Printed in Ireland with Print Procedure Ltd
Typesetting and cover design: Anú Design
Front cover image © Eoin Hennessy Photography

This story is dedicated to my little sister, Lisa.

You may have been younger than me, Lisa, but you taught me so much. I've learned so many lessons from having you in my life and I'm blessed to call you my sister.

Thank you for being the most amazing, wonderful, funny, kind human being I've ever known. I will cherish our memories and there will never be a moment that goes by that you're not in my thoughts. There's not a day that goes by that I don't hear your laugh or see your beautiful, beaming smile. I feel you left a part of you behind to be with us all, so that we can carry on with happiness and joy in our hearts.

I love you with all my heart and I promise to always be a vessel for you and carry you with me forever, until the day comes that we meet again.

Angela Doyle-Stuart
October, 2012

Contents

Acknowledgments

Thank you Lisa for being my sister and being the most incredible young woman I've ever known. I love you so much and cherish all of our beautiful memories.

Mammy, I know you're always there and I know, one day, we'll meet again. But, for now, I love that you and Lisa have each other. Thanks for being the best mother. I love you so much.

To my husband Stephen, my rock, without all your love and strength I would be lost, you have been there for me in my darkest hour and have constantly shown me the light. I love you very much.

My beautiful son, Stephen, my reason for laughing every day, you are my blessing and I thank God for you every day as, without you, I'm not sure life would be the wonderful journey it has become.

My siblings! Jane, you are the bravest woman I know and, even though there are only a few years between us, I still look up to you and cherish what we have as sisters – I would be lost without you. Catherine, you make me laugh, you have a great way at looking at life, such love and optimism, and we'd be lost without you. Michael, you are a lovely soul, you have a deep kindness in you and you never judge, you're just always there if you're needed, and I thank God you're my brother, you're the best. Rosaleen, even though we live miles apart and don't get to see each other often, I love having you in my life and I am really happy you're my family. Susan, while we have just found each other, it feels as though we were never apart and I love that you're now part of my life and that you're my family.

My father, you've had to endure what no father should ever have to go through, but you've remained strong and held it together. I'm very proud of how you've handled yourself since Lisa's passing.

My eldest nephews, Christopher and Justin, and all my nephews and nieces, you fill my days with joy. My extended family, Keith, Martin, Daniel and Margaret. My family-in-law, Ann and Gerry, I couldn't ask for a better mother- and father-in-law and greatly appreciate your support. My brothers- and sisters-in-law, Therese, Majella, Gerry, Tommy, Owen, Rachel and Bernard.

My extended family on my mother's side and father's side, there're too many to name all of you but you know who you are! However, I have to name a few as we've all grown up together: My Johnson cousins Natalie, Lisa, Laura, Kirsteen, Edward and Jimmy, along with my Uncle Ned and my Aunt Breda; my Aunt Liz and Uncle John Cook and cousins Tania, Sharon and Kim; my Aunt Loll and Uncle Jim, my cousins Teresa, Karen and Susan. My father's brother, Michael, and all the extended Johnson and Doyle families.

The people in the Bagenalstown, Leighlinbridge and Callan areas who have been a wonderful support to us over the past few years and who I am very lucky to call my friends.

My close friends – I was going to name you individually but I was worried I'd leave someone out and I didn't want that! So, ye all know who ye are and I feel so blessed to have ye in my life.

People who have helped my family along the way since losing Lisa – like Father Paddy Byrne, Liam Somers, Rita O'Quigley, Kay Spillane, Michael Lanigan, Sergeant Mick Slein, Detective Brendan Murphy, the lovely colleagues Lisa worked with in the Argos branch in Carlow and the retirement home in Leighlinbridge. Thank you all for your support.

Liam Hayes and his wonderful wife, Anne, my editor and publishers who, thankfully, understood exactly how I wanted to tell Lisa's story and offered me such kindness and understanding.

Angela Doyle-Stuart

Contact Angeladoylestuart@gmail.com
Support After Homicide (seven days a week contact): 087 983 7322.

Prologue

The Doyle family Impact Statement as read to the Central Criminal Court in Dublin, October, 2010, by Angela Doyle:

"I've had this dream for the past year where I'm walking with my little sister, Lisa, through a forest. We're linking arms and laughing and joking as we always have. We're reminiscing about our past and hopeful about our future.

We're talking about the names we have chosen for our future children, and we're laughing at what we'll be like when we're two old little ladies, looking back on the good old days.

However, as we go further into the forest I sense none of this will happen and we hold onto each other, tighter and tighter, and then Lisa looks at me. She smiles that beautiful smile, and then she's gone.

Each time I've thought of this dream, I always felt the same. How these things should have been our future; the good days, the children, the laughter.

We should be allowed to want something so precious and yet so simple. But, now, that's only a dream.

While many got to know Lisa in her 24 years, no one knew her quite like her family. She had an extremely close bond with each one of us that was very unique. She was our blessing, our gift, and we adored her.

Lisa, while full of beautiful innocence, please let that not be mistaken for gullible. Because my little sister had more depth to her than anyone I've ever known. Lisa's kindness and love for others was pure genuine. Just being in her presence would lift your mood and brighten a dull day.

Her laughter alone would have you in stitches, before you had heard the joke. Lisa was a beautiful poet, a brilliant athlete growing up and, above all, a great believer in helping others. Over the years, Lisa raised money for many charities and went above and beyond for those who needed her.

To imagine our lives without Lisa in it is just unthinkable. Every day we miss her. Her smile, her laugh, every single part of her. The world without Lisa is certainly a lot darker.

But Lisa will never be gone from us, her family.

Lisa's light will shine brightly through us, and we will continue to be her vessel, and her flame will never be put out. We have been robbed of Lisa's physical presence but we will always have her spirit."

CHAPTER 1

On the morning of Sunday, September 20, 2009, my life and my family's life was about to drastically change forever.

You know that phone call you dread? The one in the middle of the night, or that unexpected call that comes early on a Sunday morning? When you see the caller ID you know, instantly, that something's wrong.

That's how it was for me. Maybe, most people don't react to calls that way but, for me, they had become an ordeal since my mother died. I had received that awful phone call telling me about my mother's death and, now, my instincts told me this would be the same.

My mother had died seven years before, but the memory of it all was still very raw. It was a Wednesday evening, December 11, 2002. I was living in Dublin with my baby sister, Lisa, at the time. We were both working there, I was in the music industry and Lisa worked in a popular hair salon.

That Wednesday evening, at 8.30, the call came from my sister, Catherine. Her voice shook me to the very core. Mammy had died from Sudden Adult Death Syndrome. She was only 53 and she was the centre of our universe.

Now, seven years later, just before I answered this call, I felt a panic set in. Bile was rising up in my throat. A real sense of fear was already forcing me to hold my breath. It was 9.30am. Catherine asked me where I was.

I told her I was in bed, it was my lie-in day.

Catherine then gently told me to get dressed. She said that my father, brother and her partner, Martin, were coming down to my apartment. They had to tell me something that she couldn't say over the phone. Catherine said they would be with me at any minute and to get dressed and be ready to open the door.

I immediately knew something was terribly wrong. However, I had no idea it was linked to Lisa in any way. I knew Catherine and Lisa had been out socialising the night before and I had texted them on Saturday morning telling them to have a great night and that I loved them. I was too tired to make the journey up to join them that night and, strangely enough, I couldn't shake an unsettling feeling I'd had all that evening. So, instead, I had opted for an early night in.

I knew Lisa hadn't been out in weeks. She was living out in the country with Ger, her fiancé, and saving for their wedding and, on top of that, a move into their new house had taken up all her time. The house brought Lisa back closer to her family and to one of her favourite villages, Leighlinbridge. Catherine and Lisa had arranged a girls' night out there. However, it turned out that Ger wanted to go out that night, too.

Not content to let Lisa out on her own he had accompanied her. In fact, he never let Lisa do anything on her own, they were always joined at the hip. However, that night was a little different, according to Catherine. Ger had seemed anxious every time Lisa was out of his sight, asking Catherine's partner, Martin, where Lisa had gone every time she went to the bathroom or when she went to chat to her girlfriends.

But, according to Catherine, Lisa was her usual fun-loving self and seemed oblivious to any of this. She was talking to her friends and people she hadn't seen in a long time. One couple Lisa and Ger were chatting to had just got married abroad and Lisa commented on how that was a great idea, as did Ger. They both liked the thought of going away to get married and then coming home afterwards to have a party.

In their statement to Gardai, the couple recounted the full conversation they had had with Lisa and Ger. They also said how they had looked like any young couple, excited about their future, about tying the knot and making new plans.

Catherine and Lisa enjoyed their night as they chatted about family, the upcoming ploughing championships and just girlie chat in general. Lisa, not being a big drinker, had had just a few but was having fun. Catherine and Lisa finished their night off by getting some food in the local takeaway just after 1am. The two of them then made plans to meet up during the week before hugging each other goodbye. Neither Lisa nor Catherine knew that that would be their last time to hold one another.

Earlier CCTV footage had shown Lisa and Ger coming over the bridge at about 9pm, holding hands and laughing like any happy couple. Unfortunately, there was no clear footage of them walking home that night.

Five or ten minutes might have passed between that phone call and the car actually pulling up outside my home but to me it felt like hours. Inside, I had rushed around the apartment and Steve, my fiancé, had gently told me to calm down.

"I can't…" I shouted. "I know someone's either in a bad way … or dead … I just know it."

Why else would Catherine call me early on a Sunday morning? I already knew how hard that phone call must have been for Catherine.

She would have hated having to make it and would have wanted me to be up and ready, to be prepared, yet she wouldn't have wanted to break devastating news over the phone. She would have known that I would not want to hear something bad over the phone, not again. It was different when Mammy died. We had no choice.

I knew that Catherine would have felt it was important for some of my family to be with me when I was told what had happened.

By now, I couldn't really feel my hands and my mouth was very dry. I was also experiencing a cold sweat.

I took my phone out to call the rest of my family, to try to find out if anyone else knew what was going on. I tried everyone but all their phones called out, except Lisa's.

Lisa's phone went to message minder.

I even tried Ger's phone. No one would answer me so, full of panic, unable to sit still and unable to wait for the knock on the door, I threw on some old clothes, I didn't take time to brush my hair or wash my face, I just went outside to wait for the car to pull up.

Despite my fears, I never thought I would be hearing the worst news of my life.

The street was eerily quiet at that time with only the sound of my heart beating loudly and too fast in my chest. Steve was standing beside me, knowing not to speak. He could see I was too worked up. Then the car appeared.

As it was pulling in, I could see my father and brother sitting in the back seat and they looked in bad shape. They both looked pale and drawn and there was a great sadness etched across their faces. Neither of them were looking at me.

As soon as the car stopped, Martin jumped out. My father and brother, Michael, were too weak in their grief to even move. It felt like slow motion and, looking back, I realise there's no right way of letting someone know something so awful and terrible. There's a guide on how to break news to a loved one on a passing but, when family are telling each other, nothing can prepare you for how to tell the news, or what's right or wrong. And, anyway, all those handbooks go out the window.

"Tell me," I said to Martin.

"Tell me ... what's after happening?" I had the courage to ask the questions but, at the same time, I felt so ill at the thought that something so very bad had happened. Martin then said the words that would break my heart in two.

"Lisa's dead!"

Those two words came out of his mouth.

The pain I felt was unreal. Instantly, I felt like I might double up. I felt like lying down on the ground. But, Martin had something more to tell me.

"They think Ger did it," he added in a low, broken voice.

Ger O'Hara?

Ger O'Hara was Lisa's boyfriend. He was her fiancé. They had been together for five years. I don't know what I had been thinking in those few seconds. I had been thinking that maybe Lisa had been in a car crash but never, never in my worst nightmare, would I have thought he had killed her.

Lisa had loved him.

I stood there. Frozen. Confused. Terrified. None of us are programmed to think at times like that. We are never prepared for the unthinkable. Still standing outside, as Steve held me, all of the worst, the most horrific thoughts imaginable went through my mind.

My poor, beautiful, baby sister, only 24 years old, was lying lifeless and alone in the rented home in Leighlinbridge she had just moved into a few weeks before.

In those minutes, people were either going to or coming from Sunday Mass. At the time, I lived across from a church and one person, who was full of concern, asked Martin if I had been hit by a car, my pain was so visible for all to see. I wanted to die in those first few minutes. I wanted it to be me, not Lisa. I would have done anything to save Lisa even a moment's suffering.

Knowing that I had not been able to protect her was devastating. It consumed me. I was only five years older than Lisa but I still felt I would have taken Lisa's place, there and then, so she would be okay. She was too young to die. She had everything to live for.

I also wanted it to be me because, at that moment, I felt that I would never ever survive the sheer devastation of Lisa's death. I truly felt my life was over, all our lives were over and had been taken. What was the point in living? Steve tried to hold me and bring me back inside the apartment but I didn't want that. I wanted to go with my family to Leighlinbridge where my sister Catherine lived – and where, in the past, we would all congregate for family events. But now, in Leighlinbridge, Lisa was lying dead only two minutes away from Catherine's house and, somehow, the idea of being closer to Lisa was all that mattered.

Steve put me into Martin's car along with my father and Michael, who were sitting there in silence. Nothing could be said. Their voices had already been silenced by the shock. I asked Steve to follow me to Catherine's house but I told him that I first needed to go there alone.

On the drive up from Kilkenny to Leighlinbridge there was a news programme on the radio. The broadcaster was saying that the body of a young woman had been found in Leighlinbridge, Co Carlow. He said the gardai were treating the death as suspicious. A man had entered Carlow Garda Station in the early hours of the morning and was now being questioned, the broadcaster concluded.

We listened.

No one said anything.

"This can't be happening," I said aloud, but quietly and to myself, over and over again.

"This can't be real."

Over and over, the same few words came out of my mouth. I was in a nightmare but I was able to speak out loud, though I didn't know what I was saying or to whom I was saying it. I wanted to wake up but I knew I was already awake. The 20 minute car journey felt like it was taking a lifetime. My body felt racked by pain. I looked around at my father and brother and I knew I needed to be stronger.

Six months before Mammy had died, my father had suffered three massive heart attacks. Her death had being so sudden. Her sudden loss was such a cruel, heartbreaking time for us all and we had been shaken to the very core at her passing. So I knew how fragile my father had been and still remained. If only for him I needed to have a brave face.

Michael, who was Lisa's constant companion with only one year between them, had a very strong bond. Lisa had the ability to put Michael in a great mood any day and they were best friends. I was so worried about Michael. He had lost his best friend and confidante, how would he survive? I thought of everyone on that drive. How would any of us survive?

As we approached Leighlinbridge I was desperate to get out of the car. I could see Catherine standing out in the front garden and I ran straight to her. We hugged each other and said, again and again, that this could not really be happening. Catherine looked as pale and drawn as I did and she was struggling to find the words to express her sorrow and shock. My nephews, Chris and Justin, came out of the house to meet me and their beautiful eyes were so dark and red from crying.

Lisa had been like a big sister to the boys and they loved her company. I wanted so much to make them feel better but, at that time, nothing could be said to ease their suffering, as nothing could be said to ease mine.

It had only been a few hours since Lisa had died but word was starting to filter through to other people. I was beginning to receive calls and messages from concerned friends and colleagues who hadn't heard the full story but had heard some details. I didn't know what to say to them so, instead, I went inside the house to where Catherine was.

"I know it's not going to help," I told her, "... but, I need a drink."

I had never been a big drinker. On nights out I'd have been perfectly happy not to touch a drop. But, at that moment, I needed something. Something to numb me further.

I was feeling dazed and confused and was not fully registering what was happening. I looked around Catherine's house which was full of people, people just trying to make some sense of the madness and doing their best to help and ease our suffering. Aunts and uncles were there and other people that I hadn't seen in a long time. People were hovering, making tea, sandwiches, doing the usual helpful tasks. One of the local publicans in Bagenalstown, where our family originally lived, arrived with soup and food, asking if there was anything else he could do to help.

The local parish priests from Leighlinbridge and Bagenalstown were there, each knowing there wasn't much that could be said. But one lovely priest, who had been very close to Lisa, was saying what a wonderful girl she was. How she would call in for a chat with him and they'd drink tea and have lovely deep talks on God and life. How Lisa had such a strong spiritual sense and belief. Hearing that actually gave me some comfort.

My father was there, sitting at the kitchen table. And Aunt Breda, who was such a great help, was giving him tea, encouraging him to eat something to try to keep his strength up. He did so in an automatic way, not really tasting anything but too weak to refuse her offer.

My brother, Michael, was sitting on the couch in the sitting room, his partner, Mag, holding his hand, not saying anything. My sister Catherine was answering the door to all the people who called and thanking them. Chris and Justin, my eldest nephews, were like me, just wandering around in a daze unable to sit still.

Jane, our eldest sister, was on her way down from Dublin. I just wanted nothing more than for all of us to be together, minding each other. No one drifted too far from the others, the comfort we took from each other's presence was all we had at that moment. We were all too aware that Lisa, the greatest joy in our family, was not going to walk into the room as she had done only one week before.

The previous Sunday, just one week earlier, had been so different.

It had been a beautiful sunny day, full of promise and wishes for the future. Lisa and I had spent the afternoon together, chatting about future plans. Lisa was talking about planning her wedding that following summer, on June 22, and was excited about becoming a mother sometime in the future. We were both talking about our dreams.

Now, suddenly, the memory of that Sunday felt cruel. I was brought back to the present. No longer would I have those chats with Lisa.

The sorrow I felt consumed me and I felt I needed to be alone. Loads of people were coming and going and I was so swamped in grief I didn't want anyone touching me, hugging me or even talking to me. I understood everyone meant well and could see how lovely everyone was who offered their support but I couldn't take it.

I went outside into the back garden and, though it was a sunny day, I was freezing as I sat there on the bench. I lit a cigarette. I'd quit smoking years earlier, but that Sunday I must have smoked 30 cigarettes, one after the other, and I didn't care who commented or what anyone thought.

After an hour, or maybe more, when I couldn't really cope with just my own company any longer and felt tortured by thoughts of

Lisa's last moments, I went back inside to join the others. The TV was on. Everyone was just sitting around, looking at the television screen. On the RTE news we saw his face as he came out of Castlecomer courthouse in Kilkenny.

Ger O'Hara had turned himself in at Carlow Garda Station a couple of hours after killing Lisa, at around 5am. The reporter said he had been officially charged with the murder of Lisa. Still reeling with the shock, no one in the room said anything.

This was all very real, yet we couldn't fully digest it. To us, Lisa's death was still only sinking in and was still impossible to process. Even seeing him there didn't seem right. It was so surreal, it still felt like we were watching a horror movie. At the same time, voices in our heads were telling us that this had really happened and that Lisa was gone.

I didn't hate him at that moment, which may sound strange. Perhaps, I still didn't believe he had actually done it, perhaps because I didn't believe it had really happened. It was much later before I realised that it was all real, that this same man had sat opposite me and Lisa the week before in their rented house in Leighlinbridge.

Looking back on that day in their house, I suppose he seemed more odd than usual. He wasn't welcoming or friendly towards me but, then again, I had begun to see his slightly odd behaviour in the previous year as normal. He never really said a whole lot at any time. Yet, that day, when he and Lisa sat with me, he seemed tense. There had seemed to be a wedge between them, a distance, like they were sitting beside each other but they could easily have been complete strangers. I had commented on it later that day to my brother, Michael. I told him how there didn't seem to be a connection between Ger and Lisa and that the atmosphere had been really odd. Now I thought, What a difference in a week? He's gone and turned all our lives upside down, probably destroyed them, and taken the most precious person in our lives and for what reason?

Steve arrived as I was in the middle of my thoughts and he

sat down beside me, holding my hand, not saying anything, just comforting me in the only way he could.

The whole family was there in Catherine's house, consumed by grief, but poor Jane, our eldest sister, was still on her way from Dublin with her husband and son. She would have the awful task of first going to Laois hospital to see her baby sister in a way no one should ever have to. Jane had to identify Lisa's body because the garda sergeant had advised that our father shouldn't do it. My father wanted to go to Lisa but he accepted what the sergeant said.

Jane called me right after she had seen Lisa and I have never heard her so angry in all my life. There was also an overwhelming sadness in her voice, as the words came down the phone, telling us how Lisa had looked. I will always feel terrible for Jane that she had to do that alone.

"Angela ... our father would have had a heart attack there and then," Jane told me. "If he'd had to identify Lisa, there's no way he would have made it out of the hospital in one piece."

Lisa had looked so bruised and so dishevelled and hurt that Jane had asked whether or not we'd be allowed an open coffin. That was enough of an indication of how Lisa looked without us ever really knowing.

The sergeant, Mick Slein of Leighlinbridge, had been the one to break the news to my father and Catherine, and he had become a great family support. It was he who assured Jane we would be able to be with Lisa up to the final moments, explaining that there were ways and means to make it less traumatic for us to see her.

Unfortunately, Jane would have to live with the real image of Lisa in her head, an image she said she could never really tell us about.

When Jane viewed Lisa she noticed that she still had her eye make-up on, as it was glittery, and the eyeliner was still evident. I was surprised by this. It dawned on me that Lisa must not have had the chance to take her make-up off.

Lisa had studied beauty therapy and she'd often warned me, "Don't leave your make-up on at night, Angela. It adds seven days to your face!"

Lisa's advice stayed with me. After any night out, I would always make sure I washed my face, her voice echoing in my mind. Lisa herself was religious about washing it off every night. However, for some reason, this time she didn't get the chance. It's odd how these things enter your mind at such a time but I kept wondering, What had happened when they got home? What had happened to prevent her from even washing her face?

I had been in her house only a week before, so I had a clear picture in my head of what Lisa's last movements might have been. The bathroom, which was right beside her bedroom, was full of her cleansing and facial lotions. Surely, she would have washed her face before going to bed?

She had lots of cosmetics and skin care products which she had displayed for me only seven days before. I used to love how Lisa would berate me about my skincare regime on those nights when she stayed over with me during her beauty therapy course in Kilkenny. As I lived in Kilkenny, it was sometimes easier for Lisa to stay with me rather than go back home to Bagenalstown, late at night.

During those visits she would educate me on the importance of cleansing and moisturising the skin and how important things like sun protection factor and eye creams were. I loved when she came to stay. On Thursday nights, after her course in Kilkenny, we'd go out together. The majority of those times we wouldn't even drink alcohol, we'd just go out socialising and catching up. All these memories flashed through my mind and I just kept thinking, I'll never get to do those things ever again with Lisa. It was all too sickening and final.

I was beginning to feel some anger towards Ger at this point. Anger because he had robbed us all of future moments with Lisa.

At the same time, I started to fear that I'd lose my memories of my loving times with Lisa! When someone is taken from you, all you have are precious memories and I was really scared I'd lose them.

Feeling the need to hear Lisa's voice I took out my phone and listened, over and over again, to her voicemail. I listened to the lovely, kind tone in her voice. Maybe I was hoping she was still only a phone call away. Of course, that hope didn't last long and the awful reality of the day repeatedly overpowered every other thought.

I looked around at the walls in Catherine's house, at all the family pictures, we were such a tight unit. Now, one of us was gone and it made me feel so small. We were each so different and yet all so together with each other.

Each of us had our different family roles. Lisa's was always the comical one. She had this amazing ability to make us laugh even in the toughest situations and I just kept thinking, Who will make us laugh now? Is it even possible to laugh again? Will there ever be a feeling of joy again? Lisa was so like our mother. They had a great way about them that was so natural – when they told stories you'd laugh from start to finish. Now we didn't have any of that.

Then, on the very same day, several reporters came calling. One of them – I'll never forget – wanted us to talk. I swear, I hated my profession as a journalist more than ever that day. He was so quick and too cold for my liking. Some people should never be sent to call to a person's door in their grief.

The reporter got nothing and then he shoved his business card into my shirt pocket. I don't know what happened to that card but I wish I had it today.

I was too vulnerable then, we all were. Another reporter, who I felt overstepped her mark, started to tell me how her father had just died so she knew how I felt. As I listened to her, I thought to myself that my mother had died but that had not helped me to understand any of my feelings or emotions surrounding Lisa.

However, for every bad experience there're always some very kind and caring people who are respectful enough to understand boundaries and know, instinctively, the sensitivity which is needed at such a harrowing time. It would be a year later that I would learn more about the Press Council and how people, at such a vulnerable time, can be protected from this type of behaviour.

As a journalist, I would come to understand more than ever how important it is for families to be allowed to grieve in peace, and why they shouldn't be hounded or caused extra stress – regardless of the nature of the story.

Feeling more restless as the day wore on, I needed to get away to clear my head a little. I found myself heading into Bagenalstown with Steve, to my Cousin Laura's house. On our way we had to pass No 4, High Street, Leighlinbridge, the last place Lisa would live.

The Gardai were outside and I told Steve to stop the car. I went over to one of them, who was lovely, and I asked if I could go inside and see Lisa. I wasn't thinking clearly. All I wanted to do was hold my little sister. Of course, she had already been taken to the hospital and they were just preserving the scene.

They were really caring, though, and I could see on their faces how difficult it was for them to be faced with a family member in all that grief. One of the guards told me how Lisa had served him in the Argos store in Carlow where she worked, the week before. He said she truly was the friendliest and most welcoming girl and he said he felt saddened and shocked by it all. I thanked him and walked away.

After going to Laura's house where I had a quick shower to try to make myself seem more normal, it wasn't long before darkness descended and we were on our way back to Catherine's. The house was getting quieter now and Jane had arrived. She was just as shaken as we all were, even more so having been the first to see Lisa. She was the bravest person to do that.

The remainder of the day consisted of dreading the night that lay ahead. At night you're alone with your own thoughts and there's no escape.

I also knew that each day that passed would bring us closer to the day we would finally see Lisa in a coffin. I would see my little sister for the last time and we would all have to say our goodbyes.

None of us slept that night. We were haunted by the pain and images and we all had our own fears. Sleep would not come.

The next morning I was given the task of buying clothes for Lisa's burial.

CHAPTER 2

The following morning I had the task of choosing the last outfit Lisa would ever wear. Everyone felt I'd be best to pick something lovely for her as they knew we were both into fashion – me being a fashion and beauty writer and Lisa being involved in modeling.

So, not having slept for more than two hours the night before, I got up early with Steve that Monday morning and we talked about where we would go shopping. The last thing I wanted was to be going from shop to shop. I knew that that would be beyond me, it would be too much.

Walking down the familiar streets of Kilkenny that morning I felt as though I was in New York or some strange, foreign city. Each street seemed noisier, crazier and scarier than ever before. I decided I would shop at a store that Lisa had worked in years before, on High Street. She had loved working there at weekends and was loved by the girls she had worked with, in particular, the manager, Shauna, who was still employed there.

It was still early morning when we got to the store and it was perfectly quiet inside. I walked in the front door feeling extremely tense and anxious but Shauna came out to greet me. She had just found out about Lisa and had been crying. When we looked at one another, Shauna ran over to hug me. We were both grief stricken and we said very little to one another but, eventually, I told her that I needed to find something for Lisa to wear. Shauna knew what I meant. She didn't ask any questions. She knew that I could not make myself say that it was for Lisa ... for Lisa to wear in her coffin. I could not force myself to say that final word.

Lisa loved pinks and purples and I wanted her to have something pretty. I chose a beautiful dark pink dress that went up high on the neck.

During my time in the shop, my sister Jane called to tell me that we would need a scarf to put around Lisa's neck. I chose a beautiful multi-colored scarf, with stunning designs, which was made from a very lightweight material.

While I knew Lisa's legs and feet would be covered, I still didn't want them to be cold. That's all I could think about. Whether it made sense or not, I did not care. Lisa was my little sister and I wanted to do everything I possibly could do for her, even now.

I bought leggings and a beautiful pair of flat, grey pumps, with different colored diamonds on the toes. Lisa always loved diamonds and would wear the little face diamonds on a night out. It was so important to me, as I slowly walked around the shop, to find clothes and items which Lisa would have chosen to wear.

She had wonderful style. No matter what she put on she would always add her own creative touch to it. I remember giving Lisa some clothes I hadn't wanted any longer and, when I saw them on her, I didn't even know they had once upon a time been mine. For a start, Lisa always looked better in the clothes! But, also, she would add maybe a new accessory or a piece of fabric to make the essential difference. Sometimes, it was simply her natural beauty in whatever she wore that added that special something.

I thought back to the fashion shoots we had done together in the past. Lisa was always such a natural and beautiful model. However, she was never vain or aware of that beauty. She just enjoyed photos and clothes and, basically, having fun. Those days were great because they meant I got to spend time with my little sister. After the shoots we would always enjoy lunch together and have a good chat.

When she met Ger O'Hara and started to get more serious about the relationship, Lisa told me that she had no interest in doing modeling any more. Only once did she go back to it, for a charity fashion show because she knew that she could not let down the people who were working for such a good cause.

I never said anything to Lisa about her decision to stop modeling but I felt that he was playing a hand in her decision-making and that her loss of interest in doing something she had so loved was down to him. Nevertheless, as far as I was concerned, if Lisa was happy with her decision, then that was all that mattered.

Buying her last item of clothing had really awoken the memories I held and it was really hard – it was crushing. I took the clothes and paid for them and thanked the girls. Steve and I left for Bagenalstown.

That day I felt like the living dead, I felt that I was just a shell of a person and that there wasn't anything joyful left inside my body. I cried and cried, thinking of my little sister being dressed for the very last time in the outfit I had just chosen.

How I just wanted her to be warm enough. To feel good and look perfect – all those things that, in reality, were no longer important to her.

I had to drop the clothes off at the undertaker's house, Mrs Somers in Bagenalstown, who was so full of love and kindness for me that day. She had known Lisa and said how much she thought of her. She recalled how, when Lisa and her friend, Louise, had been younger, they would come into her boutique in the town and dance and sing for her and the customers. Mrs Somers remembered how her bubbly nature was always there for everyone to see and how she brightened up everyone's day.

I left realising that Lisa had known everyone, people of all ages, and how much she had meant to others as well.

I got back into the car and we drove to Catherine's in Leighlinbridge. I wanted to let everyone know what I had chosen for Lisa and explain to them how she would have loved it.

At this stage, all the newspapers had broken the story of Lisa's death. People were now calling to the house in large numbers and the phone kept ringing and ringing.

It was Monday and Lisa wouldn't be buried until Thursday. We were kindly told by our priest, Father Paddy Byrne, that we didn't have to rush anything, that it was important we spent as long as possible with Lisa.

And he was right.

Jane and I were asked to pick out Lisa's coffin, something we did in a state of semi-consciousness. We just did it. If we had thought about what we were doing we would both have broken down. It was something very important that we had to do, that's what we told ourselves. And we told one another that we were doing it for Lisa. The funeral director, Liam Somers was a pure gentleman and Father Paddy held my hand the whole time as Liam walked us through the different types of coffins.

We looked around in the room for a little while and then, in unison, Jane and I said that we'd seen the one – a pale, wooden coffin with purple on either side. It was the right choice because Lisa loved purple.

In the final seconds, as I stood and stared at the coffin we had selected, I felt sickened to my stomach that the box in front of us was actually for my little sister.

For me, the hardest part would be seeing Lisa for the first time since her death and knowing that it would be my last time with her.

I had seen my mother waked seven years before, but my mam had looked so peaceful and a lot like herself at the end. She had died in her sleep, so maybe that was the reason she looked calm.

Before we went to see Lisa in her coffin in another room in the funeral home, Father Paddy said he wanted to speak to us, to help prepare us for what was to come. I suppose Jane was, in some way, prepared having identified Lisa earlier. The rest of us tried to steel ourselves. I innocently imagined Lisa would look exactly like herself. As though she were asleep.

"That's not Lisa out there, Angela," Father Paddy told me, as if he had been reading my mind.

"She's not going to be exactly like you remember her," he continued. "And remember, she's with God now ... and she's also with your mother.

"So, when you see Lisa's body, remember, that she is at peace."

I looked at Father Paddy.

No, I thought to myself. I'll be okay. It's fine.

Of course, when the door was opened and we walked into the room, the shock was overwhelming.

Lisa looked a lot different. I wondered had the muscles changed in her face. I don't know, maybe it was just because I was shocked and unable to think or fully comprehend what was happening or what had happened. It was surreal.

I wanted to shake her a little and waken her.

I was struck by complete disbelief. The more I looked at Lisa, the harder and more traumatic everything became. I did not want to look at Lisa, lying there, not moving and never to move again. It was all too heartbreaking.

I had received a huge picture of Lisa from one of our photographer friends, Paula, and I put that lovely image of her up behind the coffin. I needed to concentrate my mind on that image of Lisa instead.

I had always loved the photograph which had been taken during one of our fashion shoots. In the picture, Lisa was looking at me as I was making her laugh. I wanted her to show off her beautiful, white, perfect teeth.

Lisa had worn braces when she was younger and, even years later, she would forget how beautiful her teeth were. As the photograph was being taken, I was telling her to smile, to show them off. She had the most heartwarming smile and her whole face had lit up that day as I was chatting to her. Everyone in our family loved that picture and, even though it was from a fashion shoot, it was a most natural pose and it was the Lisa we had all known and loved all of our lives.

Throughout the day, we kept a vigil around Lisa as we tried to support one another as best we could. Strangely, though, no matter how much we wanted to be there to help one another, seeing the pain and suffering on each other's faces was sometimes too much to bear and it felt easier, at times, to be apart. We would then take it in turns to be with Lisa.

During this time, people came to the house to pay their respects. It was a great comfort for the family to see people from Lisa's past, her primary school teachers, and people she had known long before, even men and women from the athletics club. Lisa had been a brilliant athlete. She was also a strong swimmer and had played rounders competitively in her early teenage years. She loved being part of the athletics club, where Jane and I had also spent many happy summers in our younger years. We were a very sporty family and loved all activities. Sport helped us to pass the time growing up in a small town but, more than that, it had all been so very enjoyable. Lisa was great at looking after herself and she stayed in great shape, even when she gave up competitive sport. It always showed.

As the day wore on, I quickly discovered that I wasn't coping very well. I was so full of anxiety that I couldn't sit still. The others in the family had children to look after which helped distract them, if only for a few minutes at a time. I wished I could think of someone or something else, just for a second or two.

I was dreading the funeral. The burial.

I hated that he had caused me to be like this and that his evil action had put me in such a state.

But I told myself that I was not going to allow Ger O'Hara to force me to break down completely. Seven years before, I had been in such a state at my mother's sudden passing that I had missed her funeral Mass, something for which I had never been able to forgive myself. I was present for her burial but I was too distraught to go to the Mass the night before. I know my mother would not have minded, but that huge regret had never left me, nor lessened. No member of our family had ever said anything about it, or made me feel that I had let them or our mother down, everyone had understood that I just could not cope with the suddenness of my mother's passing.

It was a few years after, that I finally accepted that these things can sometimes happen. My mother's passing had frightened the life out of me, as well. Losing a parent who was so young and from something like Sudden Adult Death Syndrome, caused an onslaught of fears and phobias that I needed to work through. For two years, I was unable to sleep properly. I felt certain that I, too, would die in my sleep.

Lisa had been my rock in those times.

I also remember her doing my hair for Mam's funeral. I hadn't eaten at all since finding out about Mam's death and Lisa was trying to get something into me and help me to relax. She was so strong. She was only 18 at the time, and the baby of the family, and yet she was minding me!

I feel she really kept me sane after Mam's passing and now, seven years on, I needed to stand on my own two feet, be an adult and be strong.

It wasn't about me. Whatever you do now, I kept thinking, you do it for Lisa.

I was asked to write Lisa's eulogy.

Trying to piece together words about her was the hardest thing I'd ever had to do. As a writer, words would normally flow easily from me most of the time but, now, I had to pray that I would be able to form words and sentences about my beautiful little sister which would do her justice. There was so much to my Lisa and I didn't want to leave anything out. Yet I knew that there was only so much I could convey in any words I would choose.

I wanted to be the one to stand up in the church and read Lisa's eulogy during the funeral but I could barely speak, even as that thought rested in my head. The ability to form a full sentence had escaped me. Thinking myself unable to function and being desperate in my instinct to help everyone in the family, as Lisa would have done, I had asked my doctor for some Valium.

I'm the kind of person who doesn't take painkillers of any kind but, for those two days, I needed something to help me cope. I knew that I had to be around hundreds of people but my grief had made me feel withdrawn. All I wanted to do was curl up somewhere safe and be alone and not wake up until everything felt normal again. I accepted that I needed something to prevent me from hiding and to help me to go out and meet people – I suppose, to allow my grief to be public. The medication numbed me for an hour or two but not for long enough and, far too quickly, and repeatedly, the pain filtered through.

Monday to Wednesday passed in a blur. The days consisted of travelling from Bagenalstown to Leighlinbridge.

While all this was going on, the O'Hara family asked if they could come to the wake. They wished to see Lisa and Sergeant Slein had passed on their request.

Our whole family accepted that we should allow them to see her. I was not in the funeral home that hour when his mother and father arrived.

It would be a year later, when we all attended court, that I would see what Ger O'Hara's family looked like, for the first time.

It was Catherine who spoke to his distraught mother. His father did not say anything and silently stepped in and out of the room. Catherine asked his mother had she spoken with Ger.

"Did he say why?" Catherine asked her.

But there was no answer to that question. And there was no way his family could ever help us find the answer which was as far beyond them as it was for any of us. I could only imagine how difficult it must have been for his mother.

She had to look at the results of her son's horrific actions. She had to stand there and look into Lisa's coffin. I'm sure those moments would be every mother's worst nightmare, more than a nightmare, something far greater and far more devastating.

The only person to blame was Ger O'Hara.

He had used his evil strength, leaving my little sister no chance to defend herself or fight for her life.

I thought back to the week before Lisa's death. Lisa and I had been together in her house and I had asked her if she felt scared there, in such an old house. I told her I would have been.

"Sure, why would I? Ain't I safe here with him minding me?" Lisa had replied to me, just one week earlier.

"And I'm never alone!" she quickly added.

Now, I prayed and prayed. I prayed in particular that that my mother had taken Lisa very early on, to wherever you go after you die, and that she was at peace, that they were at peace together. I needed to understand that they were peacefully together because, hearing Lisa's voice, over and over in my head, telling me that she had him to mind her and believing that he was her security, was more than I could cope with. I thought it might drive me mad.

My father wasn't holding up very well, during those early days. I could see how the strain had caused him to age overnight. His brother, Michael, had come down from Dublin as soon as he had heard and he had stayed with Dad and he was doing his best to keep my father from crumbling.

His brother was best for him. It felt like the rest of us were all drowning in our grief, all of us, and that none of us would be able to help one another. We all needed the voice, and physical support, of someone outside our immediate family. I had Steve. My father needed his brother. Someone, even one small step away from the immediate, painful centre of a family's grief, can offer a saving arm.

It was time to close Lisa's coffin.

It was just ourselves in the room, family and partners. I couldn't really look at Lisa. I chose to look at the photograph over her coffin instead.

Suddenly, my eldest nephew, Christopher, who had been such a strong and quiet young man, began to weep openly. Seeing the tears rolling down his face and believing that he should never have had to look upon the dead body of his beautiful, young auntie, still hurts me to this day.

We said our prayers and then left the funeral home with Lisa.

We made our way to St Andrew's Church in Bagenalstown. The town was crowded, people from near and far were standing there, on each side of the street, trying their best to offer us support. The Mass was lovely and fitting and, as it ended, people came to shake our hands. There were hundreds and hundreds of people. My arms had numbed. People I hardly knew were standing there, in public, shedding tears. People who had never met my amazing, beautiful little sister were crying. They were shedding their tears for us, feeling our grief and devastation.

That night I stayed in Nurney, not far from Bagenalstown. Myself and Steve and my friend, Fiona, who had travelled down from Meath, stayed there. Jane's husband's family owned the house and kindly offered it to me for a few days. The next day would be the biggest test of our strength.

That night with the help of some Valium, and with Steve and

Fiona by my side, I slept almost a full night's sleep. I was so thankful for this as I understood just how much energy it would take to say goodbye to my little sister for the last time.

When my mother had died, people had warned me that the burial would be the hardest part. I hadn't understood them, not until the moment came on the day we buried Mam. Now, I had some sense of what lay ahead.

Lisa's Mass was at 11am on Thursday morning. Steve, Fiona and I arrived very early at the church – I needed to be there with Lisa – but, even at that early hour, people were filtering in. I never understood, until that day, how important it is to have as much love and support around you as possible.

The last few days had really taken their toll on all of us. Throughout the service we were all trying our best to hold up. My father sat on one side of me in the top right-hand corner pew, and my brother was on my other side. Seven years before, it had been Lisa who had sat by my side, holding my hand and whispering in my ear.

"We'll be okay, Ange', Mammy will never leave us," Lisa had reassured me. "Just hold my hand any time you feel weak."

This time it was Michael who held onto me when I needed it. I have never been more proud of my little brother than I was that day. He was so devastated but, just like Lisa, he was making sure I was okay first of all.

Steve sat behind me, his hand constantly on my shoulder, making sure I could cope. Every now and then, Father Paddy would come over to make sure we were alright. He could see by our faces that we were still shocked to the core. And he could see, moment after moment during Lisa's Mass, that we were still trying to find our way. We would stand and sit and kneel, but we did not know what we had to do next. We were all living in each fine, tender moment. I remember Father Paddy telling us that we did not need to stand at any point during the remainder of the Mass. His words had come at the right time, as I could see my father finding it more and more difficult to support his own body.

Jane and my nephew, Justin, were brave enough to read a prayer each and Aunt Liz, my mother's sister, read a beautiful poem. When it came to the time for me to read out the words I had written about Lisa's life, I couldn't get up, I could not move. Father Paddy read out the passage for me. When he finished, there was huge applause throughout the church.

Later, when people came up to me, they explained how they had been unable to keep the tears at bay when hearing that Lisa would wake up in her sleep, laughing – simply because she was so happy!

In the piece, I had written about the time I had spent with Lisa the Sunday before her death, and how she was laughing so much in her sleep that I had to keep waking her up. At the time, Lisa had asked me what I had thought it meant but, before I could say anything, she answered her own question.

"It must be because I'm so happy!' Lisa said with some certainty.

To picture Lisa so happy just a few days before her death was a bitter pill to swallow. To hear her and to see her smiling face! To be with her one moment and then to have such a happy young woman snatched away from us all so cruelly!

That same Sunday, Lisa had told me that she was convinced she was seeing our deceased mother ever since moving into her new home. She had said in one incident she was washing the dishes and she had turned around and, as plain as day, Mammy was standing there, smiling at her.

Lisa said she had then blinked, stunned, and then Mammy was gone. She was convinced it had been real and now I am, too. She wondered why she was feeling Mam's presence more, and why it had started when she moved into her new house. I told her that it was probably because moves were stressful.

"Mammy is just minding you and helping you through it," I said to Lisa.

Lisa said the move had been stressful on her and on Ger.

Normally, she wouldn't have said anything along those lines but that week she told me that they had been nitpicking at each other. They were not fighting, that was not Lisa's style, but, unusually for Lisa, they had been very stressed with the move and she likened it to a divorce. She said they had moved so many times over the last few years that it was taking its toll.

She told me how one of the girls in her workplace had warned her that moving house is said to be like a divorce. I didn't push for more details that day as I didn't want to frighten Lisa off, I just wanted her to know that if she was having problems down the line she could come to me at any time, and I would be there, not judging, just listening.

If only I had known. If only I had questioned her more.

What kind of nitpicking? How like a divorce did it feel? I could have pushed Lisa for more information but, now, I will never know.

All I know for sure – and I truly believe – is that our mother was with Lisa and that Mam was prepared for the time Lisa would be taken from this physical world.

As the Mass came to an end we had chosen two of Lisa's favourite songs. Journey's 'Don't Stop Believing', her favourite song whenever she was out. Michael had chosen that for her. We also chose Sarah McLachlan's 'Angel', the song we also had for Mammy at her funeral. That was the song which played as Mammy left the church. Lisa shared the same song when she was brought from the church.

The distance between St Andrew's Church and the graveyard is about two and half miles. We walked behind the coffin, the longest walk of my life. It was a morning that might have been called sunny and lovely but I still felt only darkness. As we reached our family plot in the graveyard I started to feel panic rising in me.

All the sounds and visions around me were meshing into one and, every now and then, the ground looked as though it was coming up to meet me.

Father Paddy said his prayers, we all did. Then it was time to lay down the coffin. Whatever I had felt seven years before was completely different to how I felt at Lisa's graveside. Lisa was my little sister and she was supposed to out-live me. She was supposed to grow old alongside me.

In the future, we would share stories of our children and of our grandchildren. We would be two little, old ladies reminiscing about our lives and laughing over all our memories. We had planned on doing so much and, now, I just wanted to scream and scream.

But I knew I couldn't.

So I held all my pain inside me, with my forever-lost future plans, and, as the pallbearers gently laid Lisa and her coffin down, I was thinking how one evil monster's actions were responsible for all our pain. Watching Lisa enter the ground, I felt my own life disappear with her.

CHAPTER 3

Grief is different for everyone.

No two people feel the same and no two people deal with their emotions in the same way. Grieving over a loved one who has been murdered is, I feel, another thing altogether.

After laying Lisa to rest, we all walked away that day knowing that there would be more hard times to come, but none of us knew exactly what was ahead.

We would soon discover that we would be unable to grieve in peace during that first year. We realised, too, that, at some time in the future, we'd have to endure a trial. Little did we know it would be a one-year wait for that day and that the time in between would be so long and arduous for us all. While we mourned Lisa, we also thought about that dreaded day in the future, the thought was constantly there at the back of our minds. It was only three months until Christmas and we would all spend the day thinking of Lisa and what we had lost.

During the first year that he dated Lisa something about O'Hara didn't sit right with me.

I had planned to take Lisa on a girlie holiday after she completed her beauty therapy course and, as it turned out, he was going away at the same time. He had booked a two-week lads' holiday with one of his best friends. Our trip was for just one week.

We were leaving the day after he was and Lisa was anxious that they keep in touch throughout their holiday. As it was just their first year together, she was still in the 'honeymoon phase' and very much in love. With that came natural insecurities and the need to stay connected. He didn't seem to have the same problem. In fact, he seemed to lack those emotions but Lisa, being so full of feelings, made up for him.

It was the end of July when we went to Alanya in Turkey. He went to the Costa del Sol and, the night before our journey, Lisa spoke to him on the phone and they had worked out that they would contact each other when she was settled into the hotel. Lisa and I stayed with our sister Jane the night before the flight as she lived only a short taxi drive from the airport. We were both excited and hyper about the week ahead – just the two of us heading off.

We got up early and took a taxi to the airport. Finally, after a six-hour journey – four hours on the plane and two on a very old bus – we finally made it to our destination. It was late at night when we arrived so Lisa didn't call Ger. Instead, because we were hungry, we went for pizza and had one or two drinks. The next morning, Lisa tried calling him but his phone was off. After three days of his phone being off Lisa finally managed to get through to him and they spoke briefly. She didn't look as excited as I thought she would when she got off the phone. She actually looked concerned. She told me he was very vague on the phone and had told her that he and his friend had being socialising with a few girls from Britain and were having a great time. He'd even cut their conversation short.

I was livid at this. How dare he tell her that he was off having fun, especially since she was concerned that he had lost interest in her after he had kept his phone off for days?

I encouraged Lisa to enjoy herself and not to worry, telling her we would have fun and that they could talk when they got home. Lisa was so loyal. Even with countless admirers, she wouldn't have dreamt of cheating or even flirting with anyone, and she tried to believe that such loyalty was in others, too, even in him.

Being that bit older, I was all too aware of how badly he was behaving and I thought he was being an ass to Lisa. He had this great girl and didn't know how lucky he was. Worse, he was throwing his flirting in her face.

Depsite all this, Lisa and I managed to have a great time for the rest of the week. From funny boat trips, to manicures and hair treatments, late morning lie-ins and lots of happy chat, we really turned it into the perfect pampering girlie getaway. Though, of course, by the end of it we were driving each other mad and we were tired and ready to go home.

A day or two after we got home Lisa phoned me. She was upset and confused. She had just found out that Ger had come home the day before we had and had cut his holiday short by a week.

This really concerned me.

It was only by chance that Lisa found out. He seemed to have had no intention of letting her know.

Lisa pressed Ger for more details but, seemingly unable to cope with any probing, Ger ended their relationship there and then. Once she got past the tears, Lisa felt strangely calm and somewhat relieved that it was over. Her reaction to that breakup has stayed with me ever since.

Unfortunately, the breakup didn't last long. A few weeks later, they bumped into each other in Leighlinbridge and he convinced Lisa to give him another chance. Sadly, Lisa did.

I asked Lisa to find out if he had been seeing someone else while he'd been in Spain as I didn't want anything to come to light that could further upset her. I kept thinking, What if he has slept around? She assured me that he hadn't cheated and he had cut the holiday short because he had simply run out of money.

As far as I was concerned, things with him just never fully added up. He could never look me in the eye properly.

I remember the first time I met him as an adult was when I called up to Leighlinbridge to see Catherine and Lisa. Lisa and Ger had only been dating for a month or two. When I called in to the pub it was close to the end of the night. I wasn't drinking because I was driving so Lisa asked me if I could drop Ger home to Fenagh, about five miles away. I said, "No problem." He came out of the pub and jumped straight into the front seat beside me.

I wanted Lisa to sit beside me.

There was something about his manner, he was either flirty or leery or both, and I felt uncomfortable with him sitting so close to me. Lisa was in the back and they were both giving me directions. Not very good ones I may add, as I drove straight through a crossroads – luckily, there was no oncoming traffic!

I can't really remember the conversation which was hard to follow as they were both giddy after having a few drinks, but Lisa seemed very happy. I finally arrived at his house, after 1am, and Lisa got out of the car to chat to him and say goodbye.

They kissed and it seemed like they were well into each other. Lisa got back into the car and asked me what I thought.

"He seems nice," I said.

I found I couldn't really say much more. Before I knew it, they were serious about one another and spending all their time together.

CHAPTER

Lisa and O'Hara had been living in rented accommodation. All of Lisa's belongings were still there.

Normally, people don't go through a deceased person's belongings for a long time, months or even years, after their loved one has passed. Many people find it too painful to carry out this task, even after a long period of time. In our case, we had no option but to do so within a week.

As I had been in the house before, I knew the layout and so my brother and I went there together. None of my other siblings nor my father had ever visited the house after Lisa had moved in.

When Lisa moved into the rented house, something unusual, and out of character for Lisa, happened. Strangely, she didn't tell any of her family about the move, in fact, she was living there a full week, only down the road from Catherine, before any of us found out.

The weekend after Lisa had moved in, Catherine was having a barbecue and we were all invited. Unfortunately I couldn't attend but Lisa turned up with O'Hara. Although the rented house was only a short walk away they drove to Catherine's.

It was only later, in the middle of a conversation, that Lisa revealed that they had moved in just down the road. As far as Catherine had known, Lisa was only looking at the house. She had no idea that they had actually moved into the place.

What made this seem odd was that Lisa loved the idea of moving to Leighlin. About a week before the move, we had spoken on the phone and she'd told me that she had viewed a place and would be moving. I knew, for sure, he had somehow convinced her to keep it quiet, not to tell her family. I also felt that it showed that, if he had his way, none of Lisa's family would be invited into the house at any time in the future.

Catherine and the rest of the family were really surprised at their announcement that they had been living there for over a week and hadn't said a word. Lisa brushed it off but, apparently, looked uncomfortable. Ger was his usual mute self. In fact, it was obvious to everyone at the barbeque that it wouldn't have been Lisa's decision to wait to tell everyone because we all knew our 'Li' and knew she was super-excited about moving back to be closer to her own family.

I decided it would be best if I packed up Lisa's things myself. It wasn't easy, but I felt I had to be brave and do it for Lisa and my other siblings. My father wanted to come, too, and I asked my brother's girlfriend, Margaret, to help as well.

Going back to the scene of the murder made us all feel sick in our stomachs. We knew we had to get in and out and not think too much. I asked my father to tidy away Lisa's paintings from the walls, her television, stereo, the things that were heavy and which were all located downstairs. I felt that the less time he spent upstairs the better for him.

Gardai were there to meet us as we went in because they had keys. The landlady was sitting downstairs in the sitting room and she told me how sorry she was.

Walking up those stairs was like an eerie, out-of-body experience. To me, the house had looked dark the last time I was there but, this time, it felt even darker and incredibly bleak, there was a feeling of heavy cold energy weighing me down. I went into the bedroom and looked around. I noticed that there were no bedclothes on the bed and realised they had been taken away as evidence. I looked at the bed my sister had last slept in, in which she had spent her last night. As I stood there, anger rose within me to equal my great sadness.

When I had first walked into the bedroom I couldn't help but notice a small suitcase with some of Lisa's favourite clothes neatly packed away. Thinking it strange, I asked the female garda attending the house if the case been there when they had arrived. She said it had. I also asked the landlady if anyone could have touched anything but she assured me that everything had been left as it was.

Seeing the little suitcase with some clothes neatly packed inside surprised me. What surprised me most was that, two weeks before, when I had come into the house with Lisa and we were walking outside to admire the back garden she was so proud of, I noticed this purple hoody on the back of the kitchen door. As sisters, we swapped clothes often and I liked the hoody, so I asked her if I could have it. Lisa said no! She said Jane had given it to her and, in our family, once a sister passes on an item, it's a rule that it can not be passed on a second time. To my surprise, this hoody was neatly folded on the top of the suitcase, along with other items belonging to Lisa.

Why had she packed the case? They hadn't any holidays planned. Maybe it was because they hadn't fully moved their stuff in. I guess I'll never really know.

I checked through the items and closed the case.

Next, I went through Lisa's locker where I found personal letters, pictures and some jewellery. Of course, in the many photographs in the locker there were plenty of the two of them together. Photos of Lisa and Ger on their one and only holiday together, in Bulgaria. Lisa looking as beautiful as ever. I carefully packed away all the photos to make sure that I didn't leave any behind. I then noticed the scrapbook Lisa had been keeping for years.

In it she had photographs from her modelling days along with newspaper clippings and show pictures. She had told me that she wanted to keep all these things for when she was older, perhaps to show to her children or her grandkids. There were also letters in it but one stood out from the rest. It was from a charity, thanking Lisa for all her heartfelt work raising money for them. I was so proud of Lisa, just reading how she had helped others, something she had always done without a second thought and something she rarely, if ever, spoke about. She was such an incredibly modest and kind person.

Also in the locker, carefully folded away, was her sash from The Rose competition. Lisa had entered the local heats of The Rose of Tralee but she didn't set out to win. For Lisa, it had been an opportunity to make new friends. She had loved the whole experience of being on stage, chatting, and just enjoying her night.

On the day of the competition I had been in Dublin and couldn't make it back to Leighlinbridge until later in the eveing. I decided to call in to the Lord Bagenal Pub to see Lisa and there she was, looking as serene as ever. She was in great form and, while some people were waiting around in anxious anticipation for the result, Lisa was laughing and chatting. The result was not important to her, she didn't care. What was important was that she was having a great time and had met new people – that was enough for her.

Just as I was packing away the remainder of Lisa's belongings I noticed the ring. Her engagement ring, sitting on the locker.

Small, white gold and with a neat little diamond. She had loved that ring.

Her colleagues in Argos told me afterwards, that they would see her polishing it, she was so very proud of it. This ring had meant a commitment to their future. They were due to marry the following June 22, 2010.

Lisa was just going to have a civil service, a small intimate gathering with family and close friends. Of course, I wondered, Why not a big white wedding and invite a few more people? But she had said that was what they both wanted. She was going to have one bridesmaid – we never found out who she had chosen in the end. She couldn't wait for her big day. We were excited for her and had all offered to pitch in and help out in any way we could.

Despite being happy for Lisa, on one occasion I told Jane that I couldn't imagine marrying Ger. I asked Jane did she not think he was seriously boring. I wasn't judging him on his shyness, but Ger O'Hara just lacked something. Anyway, no matter what I thought about him, Lisa seemed really happy and I wasn't going to interfere with that or voice any negative opinions in her company.

Looking at the engagement ring, I knew we could no longer keep it. It was too closely associated with him and the false promises he had made to Lisa then robbed from her. I packed the ring into the little box and let the garda know that his family could have it and do with it as they wished.

Then I found a copy of the CD I had recorded for Steve for his birthday. I had given it to Lisa and she had loved it so much she wanted one of the tracks to be her wedding song. She had listened to the song over and over. I found the copy there in her belongings and I began to crumble. All those plans, all those wishes ... gone.

As I sat there in her room, I remembered back to the day I had gone to see her in Fenagh, where she had been staying with his family.

I hadn't seen Lisa in a few weeks and, as always, I was excited just to be catching up with her. I had the CD with me and I was looking forward to her hearing it for the first time. I had joked that she didn't have to play it as her wedding song. But she said she'd love it no matter what and she was definitely going to have it as her wedding song – Lisa was always so proud of me, as I was of her, and it could have been an awful song but Lisa would still have chosen it because of her love and loyalty to me.

On the way, I called to collect my nephews, Chris and Justin, to bring them for the drive as I knew they'd want to see their auntie, too. It was a lovely sunny day and the journey didn't take long. We finally reached the estate where his family lived.

They had a dog so, as someone terrified of dogs, I asked Justin to call at the house for Lisa. Justin called to the door. I couldn't see who answered the door but it took ten minutes before Lisa came out to us. I didn't complain, I was just happy to see her.

She jumped into the car, which surprised me a little as I thought we might get invited in. It was obvious we weren't being asked into the house but I didn't push it. So, I played the CD in the car and Lisa loved it, she said she couldn't wait to play it at her wedding. She went back into the house saying she wanted to let Ger hear it, too. A few minutes later, when she came back, she told me that he had thought it was great and was really happy with it. I thought to myself that I doubted he'd said a whole lot.

The song was called 'I'm Free', but the sad irony was that Lisa was far from free. We stayed there as Lisa listened to the song then we chatted for almost an hour, the four of us together in the car. We chatted about the wedding, about the simple but elegant dress she planned to wear and how she was trying to save for the big day: there was going to be no great socialising until she had enough money saved.

In all this time, he never came out, not once, not even to say hello to me or the boys.

I asked Lisa if he was going to come out but she said he was busy out the back, fixing the car with his father. No one came out to say hello to us and I thought it was very strange. I still didn't know what any of his family looked like and, soon, Lisa would be marrying into them.

The boys were anxious to get back to their pals so Lisa and I hugged and kissed goodbye. I told her I'd see her soon and she took the CD with her and waved goodbye as she went into the house. I drove off that day a little worried about Lisa. I was worried she might be lonely out there, I wondered why he hadn't made the effort to come out and say hello, especially as we had been there for so long.

Just as I had before, I shook the feeling off.

Sitting in Lisa'a last bedroom, I turned the CD over in my hand. The cover was slightly worn, testament to the fact that Lisa was proud of it and had loved playing it. She knew the song word for word. After Lisa had passed, I couldn't listen to the song without being reduced to tears and a deep, intense sorrow.

It's a song I stopped listening to and will never listen to again.

We eventually came towards the end of what we had to do in Lisa's house. We had all of her belongings packed away or in bags in the back of my car. We had decided that, for now, we would put it all away until the time was right for us to get together and go through everything.

After Lisa's death, I became friends with one of her former work colleagues from Argos, a lovely girl who lived in Carlow. Speaking to her about her friendship with Lisa, she told me that she hadn't liked Ger O'Hara, she'd found him odd and very possessive of Lisa.

There were a few instances when she felt unnerved by him. One occasion that stood out most for her was when she had invited Lisa into her home. The two girls went upstairs to look at something on the computer but he had followed Lisa and, when the girls turned around, he was there behind them, sitting on the bed. Lisa'a friend turned to him and said, "God Ger, you'd make an excellent stalker!"

He didn't react. He just sat there on the bed, waiting until Lisa was ready to go. This concerned Lisa'a friend because she felt he wasn't allowing Lisa any space to herself.

Another time, when she had given Lisa a lift home from work one day, Lisa refused to be dropped off at the house. In fact, when they were as much as a hundred yards away from her home, she was already getting out of the car while it was still moving. After that, Ger dropped Lisa off at work and collected her every day. The picture that was emerging was of a very controlling man.

Afterwards, Lisa's boss told us that he had been surprised by O'Hara's habit of turning up to collect Lisa an hour before her shift ended. He did this most days and when her boss asked if he had far to drive and was that the reason he came so early, Lisa had laughed and said no, he just likes to be on time.

In my opinion, he was making sure Lisa was coming straight home after work. It was the same with Lisa's swimming. He wouldn't even allow Lisa to have that to herself.

Lisa, my brother, Michael, and his partner, Margaret, would go swimming once a week and O'Hara would drive them. Michael used to offer to drive but O'Hara would insist, yet he'd never go into the swimming pool. Instead, he'd stay outside in the car for an hour or more waiting until Lisa was finished. Michael did find this odd but he had become used to Ger's strange behaviour and, as Michael doesn't go around talking about others, he never said anything about this to anyone else.

I wish I had known how controlling he had been. Maybe I would have said something, maybe we should have pieced more information together. If we had, there is more we would have known about him.

Now, I encourage all families not to ignore the little things. If someone is controlling, or manipulative or bullying then share what you know. It's important and it might even help in the life of your loved one.

I don't know whether finding out more about Ger O'Hara would have changed anything sufficiently to save Lisa'a life. He was too manipulative for that and there was no way we could have foreseen what was coming. Still, I would encourage others to take a good look at who's in your life and look at those around you. I'm not telling people to be distrustful but definitely more aware.

If instinct is telling you that something doesn't sit right or feel right then, the chances are, things aren't right. My instincts were telling me that Ger O'Hara was different and strange. I was unsure of him and so, too, were others. We could never have imagined, for a second, that he was a murderer but I do wish I had questioned his behaviour more.

I understand now, more than ever, how we all take people at face value. We're too trusting, so we automatically believe that the good outweighs the bad in people.

Tragically for Lisa, the opposite was true of him.

CHAPTER 5

Three weeks after Lisa's murder I went back to work.

I'm not sure if that was too soon, or whether or not I was ready. At the time, I was finding it difficult just being in my own company. Steve understood this and he changed his plans to be with me. He was supposed to go to Cork for a ten-week course as part of his fitter apprenticeship but, instead of moving there for the ten weeks as he had originally planned, he decided he couldn't leave me on my own and drove up and down, every day, from Kilkenny. It was that kind of understanding that really made the world of difference. Although, at the time, I had no idea how I would feel, there was no way I could have been on my own and he knew it. Without his support, I'm not sure how I would have coped.

As it was, I was so ill at ease that I couldn't enter a room at night if the light hadn't been switched on first, I couldn't be alone in my apartment, even during the day, without the TV or radio or some kind of noise to stop me from feeling so alone.

Whenever Steve got up early in the morning to leave for Cork, he'd have to turn on a light in the room and switch on the TV so that I wouldn't be scared. I was constantly jumpy. Every little thing frightened me for weeks and months afterwards.

When something unpredictable and traumatic happens in your life, it destroys your trust in everything – I had often heard this said but had never really understood until I felt it too. I had stopped trusting everything and everyone. When you don't have any trust then your life becomes a very lonely, dark place.

Unless I had to, I wouldn't leave my apartment during the day. If Steve wanted to go somewhere then I would go with him but, for a long time, I would get up early and just stay there, in my place, and not move. Being outside was too stressful. I was a ball of anger. I had lost all my patience and I knew even a walk up the street was probably beyond me. Sometimes, I'd sit in front of the TV but I wouldn't be watching or taking in what was on. I had lost all interest in day-to-day things.

I forced myself to shower. When Lisa and I had lived together in Dublin, we were so sad and devastated after Mammy's death that the smallest tasks had seemed impossible. Lisa was the one who made sure we took care of ourselves.

"Angela!" she'd say, "We can't let ourselves go. We have to shower, eat and take care of ourselves. The rest will sort itself out in time."

That was Lisa.

So, now, I thought about what she had said and followed her advice. I washed every day and managed the usual bits of pampering, anything to regain a little bit of control over my sad life.

The morning I was due to go back to work, I felt really anxious. I was as anxious as a little girl starting her first day at primary school. The memories came flooding back and I was, once again, a frightened little schoolgirl who wanted her mother to hold her hand and walk her through the gates.

Of course, that wasn't going to happen so I just prayed and asked my mother and Lisa to be by my side as I went back to work. Walking into the office that morning most people didn't say anything as I had asked them not to. I knew I couldn't stand there talking about what had happened, that I'd break down.

As a journalist, going back to work was additionally strange for me because the nature of my work would bring me into contact with the public, but, right now, I didn't want to see or talk to anybody. For some time, that was beyond me. I wasn't able to pick up the phone to do interviews or go on the street to do vox pops with passers-by. I felt very odd those first few weeks and very vulnerable. There were times, at the mere mention of the word 'death', that I just wanted to burst into tears.

I found it heartwarming, though, that so many people had contacted my workplace, dropping in letters and cards of condolence. A lot of these people I had never even met, but they were offering their words of kindness. Those letters and cards certainly made my steps lighter.

As the weeks wore on, I managed to block out my feelings and zone in on the tasks at hand and keep my life separate to work. I found it was the only way to cope. People were understanding but, at the same time, it was only perfectly natural that they should be uncomfortable with outbursts of emotion.

However, during those dark times some life-changing and wonderful events also took place. Just before my 30th birthday, on November 10, Steve proposed.

It was, as you can imagine, a bittersweet moment.

I had never felt such joy and sadness in one instant. The joy simply because I knew I wanted to spend my life with Steve and now I knew, for sure, that he wanted that as well – I remember feeling such a rush of love and happiness in those moments. But, when he held me, I cried. Tears of joy mingled with tears of sadness because I knew I wouldn't share that precious moment with Lisa.

I cried because I knew I had someone who would cherish me and protect me, and that was all that Lisa had ever wanted too. Lisa, more than anyone, deserved that.

The proposal gave us all something to focus on and the news of a happy occasion in the family was, naturally, met with a sense of relief. When people heard our news we were met with an outpouring of kindness – even people who might not have known us well were delighted to hear any bit of good news for our family. This lovely support and kindness has shown me that, for all the bad and evil in the world, there are many wonderful people out there who just wanted to ease our pain.

Christmas was only a short while away and none of us were looking forward to it. It wasn't just because we'd all be together and, perhaps, be forced to deal with one another's thoughts and emotions. We dreaded it because we would all miss Lisa.

We had felt the pain at my 30th birthday dinner, it was nothing fancy, just siblings and partners out together for a meal, but it wasn't the easiest meal to sit through. We all felt the strain, there was a lot of heaviness and unhappiness among us all. Whenever we got together as a family, Lisa's absence suddenly became very real.

When Christmas day came, it was a quiet affair spent at Catherine's house. The children occupied most of our thoughts. Although it was by no means a house full of laughter, there were no tears either. We all kept it together that day, for the children.

In the past, our family tradition had been to organise a Kris Kringle, where we put all our names into a hat and each of us pulls out one name and buys a gift for that person. None of us wanted to do our Kris Kringle that year, in fact, we haven't since. I'm not sure we ever will again. I was Lisa's last Kris Kringle and to do it now, without her, would seem unfair.

After Christmas dinner, my family decided to visit the grave but I didn't go with them. In fact, it would take me almost a year to make it there. I couldn't bring myself to stand in the graveyard knowing I had been there on many occasions with Lisa. We would walk there together, laughing along the way, giggling as we passed the house with these scary dogs that would bark like mad. Even when the dogs were locked up, we'd still act like cowards and run past the house laughing our hearts out. On our way back home, we'd go into a small cafe in the town and we'd have a scone and drink tea and just chat, happy in each other's company.

The thought that Lisa was in that grave now hurt too much. After Mammy had died, Lisa would spend a considerable amount of time there alone. She would pack her lunch and off she would go and spend hours sitting there chatting to Mammy.

When the time eventually came to visit the grave I couldn't do it alone and I asked my brother, Michael, to come with me. I didn't feel any of the comfort or peace that some people get from a visit to their loved one's resting place, I felt the cold, dark reality of finality.

I suppose, for me, it's different. I believe Lisa's around me, it's the same belief I have about Mammy, and a headstone just seems so cold and comfortless to me.

As the days passed after Christmas, our first without Lisa, I knew I was hitting rock bottom very fast and that my trust issues were taking over. It was then that I decided to call the Support After Homicide group. They had kindly approached us through the Garda Liaison Officer shortly after Lisa died, and now I knew I needed all the help I could get. I needed to rationalise what was irrational.

Rita was my counsellor. She was a kind-hearted, super, lovely woman who really helped me centre myself. Rita's warmth and advice certainly helped me. She helped me to realise that what I was feeling was completely normal and that a lot of people felt the same way after losing someone through murder. It's not normal, so it's about trying to find normality in something so abnormal and senseless.

As the rest of the world continues, time seems to stop for people who are bereaved. This can make grief very difficult to bear. You feel you want to ask everyone else to slow down, to understand what you're feeling, because it's so strange and upsetting, and you know you can't because they'd never be able to fully understand.

The first time I acted irrationally was when I was walking home from work one day. I'll never forget it, it was a Wednesday and I'd finished work at 2pm but, even in broad daylight I began to feel I was under threat from a man who was simply walking close behind me. I became convinced that he was going to try something. I felt so vulnerable that I believed he was going to attack me. I rushed home and locked the door and, after thinking it through carefully, in the quiet of my own home, I knew I couldn't continue to live my life that way. When I thought of it later that day I realised I was feeling extremely paranoid and over-cautious, but it was not my fault. The shock of what had happened was manifesting itself in different ways in my life. I was afraid it might to take over.

Like Lisa, I had always been a deeply spiritual person and I discovered that counselling was what I needed to restore a peace within myself. I had heard of people who had lost their minds after going through so much grief, I knew there were people who had ended their own lives as a result of being unable to cope with the loss. Of course, I was scared. I never considered ending my own life but I was worried that my irrational behaviour would take over and be damaging.

If my paranoia in the middle of the day was so overpowering, what might be next? So, I looked into myself – What makes me stronger than anyone else? How can I keep myself strong and sane? I knew no one else could fix me only me and, if I was going to keep my mind, I had to start sooner rather than later. I didn't share that fear with anyone other than Rita. I didn't want to make it more real.

To make a start I needed to find peace so I turned off the TV then the lights and I got rid of all the other distractions. I lay down on my bed and I began to meditate.

I didn't have a guideline, I didn't have a mantra, I just prayed. I just asked for guidance and understanding and the ability to see clearly. Gradually, in the most beautiful beams of light, I saw my fiancé, my siblings and those closest to me. The energy that surrounded me felt amazing. I looked at each peron closely and I could see how loving and deep they each were, how their hearts were full of kindness. They were surrounded only by good, no evil.

Then I saw him.

At that moment, I decided I would not allow him to destroy the rest of my life. Instead, I would concentrate on my love for Lisa, concentrate on her life and all she had been to us, and not allow him to have any part of that any more. I decided, there and then, that Lisa's life could not be in vain so I had to stop allowing him to destroy what was in me.

I would be a vessel for Lisa, I would allow her light to shine through me so that she would always be a part of me and I might, one day, be half the person she was.

After setting aside time to meditate in this way for a few days, I finally started to feel my fears and trust issues calm. I was no longer scared of the dark nor did I feel as nervous about the unknown, those things that didn't really make sense.

If I was going to get emotionally stronger I knew I needed to build up my physical strength, too, so Steve and I joined the local gym. Running and swimming offered me a way to think more clearly. The extra endorphins also gave me a little lift!

There were difficult days, though, when I was on the treadmill and I'd feel the tears start to flow and I'd have to stop myself from breaking down. But, as time wore on, I learned to keep my feelings in check and my grief more to myself.

The recurring dreams that I began to have were difficult to deal with.

I suppose when you lock your feelings up inside they find a way to come out and mine burst through into my dreams, forcing me to come to terms with what had happened. In a way, they helped to heal me.

One recurring dream was about Lisa suffering from a fatal illness. She had been given only three weeks to live and we were doing all we could to make them the best three weeks of her life. As the dream progressed, the upset and devastation the whole family felt at saying our goodbyes, and the pain of losing Lisa, became insufferable. Then, suddenly, I'd wake up. For just a split second, I'd feel a huge sense of relief that it had been a dream, only to be struck by the terrible realisation that Lisa really was gone. The reality was much worse than the dream.

The sadness I felt the mornings after those dreams seemed never-ending but I'd have to try snap out of it. I'd put in the eye drops to hide the redness, force myself to eat and go to work when all I wanted to do was bury my head under the duvet and grieve.

That's the thing about loss. In a way, the first few weeks are the easiest because you're being protected by the numbness and the shock. Gradually, the months pass and, when the numbness wears off, all hell breaks loose with your emotions. Although people are sympathetic and kind, it's hard for them to fully grasp the weight of it all unless they've experienced a loss themselves. Just a few months after Lisa's death, Steve was asked by someone he knew if I was still upset. Of course, Steve explained, as gently as he could, that grieving is a long process. Perhaps, the person didn't understand because he had never experienced the death of a loved one. A girl, who was trying to be kind, once told me, "You'll be okay in 18 months, Angela." I didn't say anything in reply but I thought, Who, in God's name, puts a time on when someone will be okay? Comments like these can get to you if you allow them to but what good would that bring? Energy is so precious when you're grieving that you can't really waste it on others.

The dreams have changed over time and sometimes they're lovely and peaceful. At other times I wake up feeling worse than ever. But at least now, while I dream, I know Lisa's dead. My mind is no longer playing tricks on me.

The sweetest dreams are the ones in which Lisa and I walk together, chatting and catching up as if she had never gone. I dream about those times because they are the moments I miss most, when we'd go for really long walks down by the river in Bagenalstown and we'd chat about everything.

Lisa was so in enthusiastic about life and everything in it. She wanted to learn about everything and embraced everything and everyone that she met. In fact, her positive nature helped her through a difficult period at secondary school when she was bullied. I always believed the bullying was born out of jealousy. Lisa was very pretty and so warm and the only conclusion was that these people were just jealous. She'd ask why people were like that, wondering if there was something wrong with her and it would break my heart because she was so far off the mark. If you knew, Lisa you could only love her.

I'd explain to her that people only bully others when they're jealous or intimidated by that person. Usually, the bully wants to be more like the person they are picking on and, when they can't be, they try to bring the innocent party down to their level.

Lisa never faltered, though. While she wore her heart on her sleeve – and what you saw was always what you got with my little sister – she had a quality in her that kept her from breaking. Those tough experiences didn't make Lisa bitter. In fact, in later life, she became friendly with those same people and never bore a grudge.

During our walks she wouldn't allow me to bitch or moan about others. She didn't believe in talking about people as she felt it was unfair when they didn't have a chance to defend themselves. On the other hand, her loyalty to her family was so strong that if anyone ever did an injustice to a loved one she'd be the first to defend them.

Lisa's kindness and openness to others shone through. Even when I was in a hurry and felt I hadn't time to chat she would stop and listen to people's stories. Just the week before we were robbed of Lisa, we had been walking through Leighlinbridge together. I, as always, was in a hurry so, when met this acquaintance who had just had a baby, Lisa had to stop and chat with her. Ten minutes later we were still there and I was waiting, impatiently, for her to finish. Such was her genuine interest in others that, no matter how great or small the detail, Lisa treated it all with equal importance. I always felt content in Lisa's company and I could clearly see she had the same effect on others with whom she mixed.

There're so many chats I wish I could have with Lisa, so many things I want to share with her.

Although that first Christmas was difficult, we were given a beautiful surprise which eased the family's pain a little.

We had always known that we had another sister, Rosaleen. She was my father's daughter, born before my dad met my mother. We knew all about Rosaleen from a very young age but, that Christmas, we met her for the very first time.

While we were still filled with sadness, as it had only been a few months since we had lost Lisa, it was great to finally meet Rosaleen, face to face. With each passing year, she has become so close to all of us. It's like we have always known each other. When my sisters and I were young girls we would write to her but to be able to sit down and talk to her, was a joyous moment for us all. It was lovely to see our family expanding and, while we still experienced a roller-coaster of events and emotions, there was also healing being offered to each of us, every single day.

CHAPTER 6

As the weeks passed, we all began to focus on our own lives, and yet none of us could forget what we had lost or what still lay ahead. Shortly after Christmas, we were given the court date of October, 2010.

That day was a huge worry at the back of all our minds but we learnt to cope and tried to live our lives as normally as possible.

I tried to keep things close with the family but, perhaps inevitably, we had all drifted apart. I suppose it might have been our way of protecting ourselves from losing someone else. Plus, it was too much at the time to talk about Lisa.

My father divided his time between our home place and family up in the north of Ireland, so it could be six weeks or longer at a time before we met up.

We all stopped texting. We stopped calling each other quite as much as we had. And, individually, as we were all trying to piece our lives together, we were unable to function normally in each other's company.

After Christmas, we didn't meet up again until the following

April. When Mammy had died we had all got really close and formed a really strong bond. Now, it felt like we were losing that bond and, while we kept telling each other that he would not ruin us and that we were still a strong family, it was, sadly, already starting to happen.

On April 24, Lisa would have been 25 years old. I decided I would bring the whole family together again and I organised a barbecue in my place. The initial idea wasn't met with great enthusiasm and I suppose some people felt it was unnecessary. What exactly were we celebrating? that was the question. However, I wanted to make sure Lisa's birthday would be something we would all make the effort to celebrate together as a family every year.

I suppose, once again, I wanted to keep Lisa alive as much as possible within all of us. Of course, the rest of the family wanted that, too, we just had different ways of going about it.

The day itself wasn't cheery and most people focussed on the children. While I still felt it had been a good idea, I could also see that emotions were still too raw for everyone. There were some silent tears shed and, by the end of the evening, I couldn't help but feel people were relieved to be leaving. I didn't blame them.

Lisa's 25th birthday was going to be important to her. She would joke that she'd be a quarter of a century old and be in the new age bracket, 25 to 40, which she was actually excited about. Lisa embraced age, it wasn't something that frightened her.

She had worked with the elderly in the retirement home in Leighlinbridge and she had loved it. She loved their stories, their wisdom and, most of all, taking care of them. Her hair and beauty therapy experience meant that she also enjoyed doing their hair and sometimes even their make-up. I remember, once, Lisa remarking that she'd love to also help them get fitter and up on their feet, but she understood that most of them couldn't manage that, they were too fragile. That's what I loved about Lisa, she only ever wanted to help others.

We all knew that on the day of her 25th birthday she should have been blowing out the candles on her cake, laughing and enjoying herself. Most of all, she should have been looking forward to all the other birthday parties she would have in the future.

The birthday barbeque was a learning experience for me. I came to understand that I couldn't force normality onto others just because I wanted to believe I was still in control. I learned that I had to give people time and hope that some form of normality would return naturally.

Perhaps, though, what I learned most of all was about myself – that I had begun to hate Ger O'Hara.

Looking back at how everyone was that day, I see that we were all broken and he was to blame. It was, for me, the darkest period concerning him. Too much anger had boiled up inside me that I couldn't deny any more. Until then, I hadn't really focussed much on what he had done and I still wasn't sure what had happened to Lisa. It wouldn't be until the days before the court case that I would learn the facts. But, maybe because I didn't have a clear understanding, I began to imagine what he had done and I felt rage towards him. I kept thinking, How dare he? How dare that monster rob us of Lisa?

And how dare he write, in a letter he presented to the Gardai, that Lisa was, "The girl he loved more than anything in this world"?

It made my blood boil. After all, you don't destroy someone you love, you nurture them, you take care of them, you protect them, none of which he did for Lisa. He didn't have the right to say he loved her because he didn't know the meaning of love – or anything approaching it.

If you're experiencing urges to murder and you know you're a risk, especially to the person you claim to love, then surely to God you go and get help? He had plenty of opportunities in those four and half years to get help but he never did and, I believe, he always wanted to give in to what he claims were "urges".

He was able to think remarkably clearly immediately after murdering Lisa. He had been drinking and I assume he took his time before giving himself up to let some of the alcohol wear off.

He was 'together' enough to walk into a petrol station and buy a notebook and pen and a packet of chewing gum.

His mind was clear enough to sit down to write a very well-written letter.

He was able to park his car, the one that Lisa had bought him, in such a way that the Gardai later said they'd never seen a car parked so well.

Strangely, after all this apparent normality, he then proceeded to act erratically in the Garda station, pulling his hair out, and crying. How strange that he was calm enough to carry out all those other tasks first.

When the gardai questioned Ger and asked why he had done it, his answers were always the same: "If I knew why I wouldn't be in this mess right now," he told them, repeatedly.

I felt sick when I heard that he had presented a note to the gardai. We initially believed it was a simple hand-written note but we later discovered it was a very well-written, coherent letter, that he had written less than two hours after robbing Lisa of her life. We finally saw it for ourselves in court. I didn't believe then that he was sorry and I don't believe it now, regardless of what he wrote in the aftermath.

Memories from the past came flooding back to confirm to me that he was too self-absorbed to put Lisa first and take care of her. My mind traced back to the times when I started to dislike him.

I thought back to the first time I had introduced Steve to him. I had only been seeing Steve for a short while and, though it was important for me that he meet my family, I wanted Lisa to be the first. I had told Lisa everything about Steve and was excited for them to meet because I knew they'd get on well. So, we arranged to go to the local pub in Leighlinbridge to meet Lisa and Ger. We sat together in the beer garden – Lisa sat across from me and O'Hara sat opposite Steve. He'd had a few drinks and was a little more talkative than usual. Steve was really taken with Lisa, how open and friendly she was, and he felt we were very alike.

So, he turned to O'Hara, as Lisa and I were just chatting, and said, "The Doyle girls are lovely, aren't they?" I just happened to catch O'Hara out of the corner of my eye. He looked really leery. He agreed with Steve that we were lovely alright and then he gestured down to his chest.

Steve changed the subject fast. I was doing my best not to say anything so I waited until we left the pub when Steve apologised profusely to me.

"God, Angela, I never meant about ye're looks, I meant how lovely ye both are," he explained. "How Lisa and you are both alike in your friendly nature. I wasn't talking about your sister's chest or yours!"

Steve felt he couldn't apologise enough.

We were both thinking that this guy had been with my sister long enough and he was old enough to come up with something a little bit better than a leery gesture. That bugged me about him. He was in his late 20s at the time, had been with Lisa a few years, and he was starting to show his true colours. That gesture showed to me that he really looked at Lisa as more of a possession, more of a trophy, rather than the beautiful person she was.

Of course, there were other similar moments, like when he wanted Lisa to model at some car shows. Lisa called me to ask for my opinion so I told her that, if it was something she really wanted to do, I wouldn't get in the way. I also told that she was old enough to make up her own mind.

I didn't like the idea of her standing there in very little clothing, basically for the enjoyment of men who were half-looking at cars. I'm not judging other girls who do this form of modelling for a living, and I'm sure they enjoy their lifestyle and are in full control, but it was just not Lisa's style. I asked her what had made her think of doing it and she replied: "Oh, Ger thinks it would be great if I did it. He'd be there with me and said I should show off my figure."

The thing was, while he was clearly possessive, he also got some sort of kick out of lads checking Lisa out, but only in his presence. I'm glad to say that having listened to my concerns, and talking to some of her co-workers, Lisa decided not to go ahead with it.

I would like to be able to tell you that I'm so spiritually evolved that I can offer forgiveness to someone like O'Hara, but I don't believe it's my place to forgive him. I will gladly live a fulfilled life without ever doing so. I have no room in my heart for him.

Now, I wake up in the mornings and I don't think of him. I think of my father who is suffering with a bad heart and who is very lost and haunted by the fact that he couldn't save his youngest child who was living less than two miles away from him.

I think of my other siblings that want nothing more than to hug their little sister. I think of all the children in the family who will never really get to know their wonderful Auntie Lisa.

I think of myself. How I miss my best friend, every single day. How, so many times I have gone to pick up the phone to call Lisa, only to be winded by the fact I can't do that ever again – and that still gets me every time.

It's the little things you lose track of and that hit you the hardest. Those little things get you at times you don't expect them to. I remember walking into town one day to meet a friend. The walk takes me 15 minutes, so I'd normally call someone to chat with along the way. Around a year or more after Lisa died I remember heading off into town and taking out my phone and thinking, Who will I call? I'll call Lisa.

It was only a split second's thought but I was left reeling, God Angela, how stupid can you be! The tears just flowed.

I thought I had got my head around it all but, clearly, I hadn't. While part of me, a large part of me, had accepted Lisa was no longer with us, the rest of me was still just catching up. As I made wedding plans I would visualise Lisa there with me in so many different places. But, each time, I had my happy thoughts dashed and my heart broken as I reminded myself that she wouldn' be there on my big day.

When he gets out of jail, I know Ger O'Hara will have the chance to remake his life but he never gave Lisa any chance. I don't believe he sits there in his cell and feels devastated by grief. I truly don't feel he is capable of any form of remorse.

What really convinces me that he's perfectly comfortable in jail is my memory of the time when he and Lisa lived with my father. They lived in my father's home for six months.

Every day, Lisa would go to work but he was not working and would sit in the bedroom all day. He locked himself into that room and didn't come out until Lisa got home.

My father would always offer him dinner, cups of tea, the usual, and he would only ever grunt in reply or say he was grand. Obviously, he was okay with the solitude, there in that bedroom, sitting, seven hours a day.

Of course, it was odd behaviour but we just didn't know enough and we weren't looking for signs of evil in him. We have learned, in the hardest way possible, that some people are good at hiding their true feelings and intentions.

I would love to believe that he, too, is suffering that he, too, wakes up in the middle of the night screaming and crying like we've done. But I don't think he shares the emotions we have. If he did, if he had anything inside him, he would never have acted like he did in the first place.

In the months that followed, I let my anger against him go, never forgetting, but not allowing it to take over my every thought.

His phone records showed that he had every other family member's number in his phone, except mine. He had tried to create a wedge between myself and Lisa. He knew we were extremely close. He knew Lisa always listened to me and he knew we had shared everything growing up. He didn't like that and I could tell – I knew he was jealous or bothered, or something, but he was never man enough to say anything to me. I suppose me being upfront and often blunt didn't help him. But, believe me, I had tried to find some good in him. I wanted to believe there was goodness there, that Lisa had seen something that she loved. I was confused by them. I asked Lisa so many times what their relationship was like. I asked her if they had normal conversations.

"Yeah, of course we do. We always chat," she told me.

But I often wonder if Lisa did all the talking.

He was too controlling and manipulative to allow his true colours to be seen. I remember at my nephew, Nathan's, christening, a few months before it happened, how I hadn't seen Lisa in a while and we were all going out for some food and drinks after. Lisa was only in the pub for about an hour before she said they were leaving. I was put out by this.

"No, you're not leaving," I told her.

"Ger wants to go home and get changed," she insisted. "We'll be back in later."

First of all, I knew that wasn't going to happen. But, more than that, O'Hara knew that I could only stay for a few hours as I had to head back to Kilkenny.

I put my foot down.

"No, he'll be alright!" I told Lisa. "Sure what's wrong with what he's wearing?"

I told Lisa it had been way too long and I wanted to catch up with her. O'Hara didn't object on that occasion because he knew I would not back down. Thankfully, Lisa listened to me and stayed and we had a good evening.

Looking back now, I'm glad I stood up in those moments and stopped him from taking them all.

That evening, Lisa and I spoke about her wedding and about the music she would have. Steve's father is in a band, so I said I would price them for her and, if not, then maybe a small three piece might be better. I said I'd do what I could to put the money towards it, as my gift to Lisa. We had a good laugh together and, in the end, we both left the pub at around the same time. While we were there, I don't recall him mingling or really speaking to anyone. Whereas Steve, who didn't really know anyone that well at the time, was walking around chatting to everyone.

As summer drew closer, so did the family. The time apart had helped and a healing was beginning. Jane announced she was expecting her second child, a boy, and this brought more happiness into the family.

Her baby was due that November, which would be a month after the court case began. Naturally, while we were all happy we'd have a new addition to the family, we were also worried about Jane and how stressful the case might be on her. But, as we had discovered, we were and are, a very strong family. I don't know any unit as strong as my family, I really don't. We've come through so much and once we got over the earlier hurdles, we've been there for each other ever since, stronger than ever.

That summer, the days seemed to fly by. Steve and I decided we would get married the following year and plans were put in place. I started to feel a slight spring in my step and I found myself laughing at things more and more and actually starting to enjoy myself.

I developed a confidence that I hadn't had before, I had started to mature and I no longer felt as insecure and unsure of myself.

Instead, I had become very comfortable in my own skin. I found the things that had upset or bothered me before becoming irrelevant and I no longer dwelled on the small stuff. I felt whenever I laughed, now, there was real depth to it. I could feel Lisa's infectious belly laughter echoing through my head and many times I felt her there with me.

There were, of course, still the dark days and I certainly tested my relationship with Steve to the limits on many of them but, in the process, I also discovered how lucky I was to have such a remarkable and understanding man. At times, Steve had borne the brunt of my anger and pain. I would lash out at him if I was having a bad day or whenever we had a couple's argument. I'd shout at him that he wasn't going through what I was, that he hadn't lost his sister.

Of course, I was just hurting and needed to off-load my pain, which Steve understood but, at times, it was unfair. He never made me feel bad about those times and was always there for me. He knew that it would pass and that, over time, I would heal. And he was right. We also knew that the trial would be the biggest test of all, not just for us as a couple, but also for me as a person.

My counselling with Rita was giving me some insight into what lay ahead for me. However, Rita repeatedly warned that nothing could fully prepare me for the day. She explained that the courtroom wasn't really a place for emotions, that it was a very cold and uninviting place.

I was dreading it. I was worried about my reaction, and that of the rest of my family, to facing him for the first time since it had happened. I had been warned that some people, when faced with the killer who took their loved one, can respond in a way that it is very out of character so there was a huge sense of the unknown for us all. We were unsure about how the day would go and we were deeply worried about it.

It would be wrong to think that I was scared of him because Ger O'Hara didn't frighten me. But, it was unsettling, and strangely painful, anticipating the trial. I knew that the trauma of a court case has often prevented the innocent parties from healing. I desperately wanted to heal. I couldn't wait another year to begin the process of dealing with my pain.

CHAPTER 7

I found the best way of healing was to delve into my memories and look back over the years I'd had with Lisa. I would write down important events and remind myself of what she had left behind in her short time with us.

It was important for me to remember that while Lisa had left so much undone, she had also achieved a lot – not materially or for her own selfish gain but spiritually.

In the darkest days after Lisa's death I remember being angry at God, and screaming, "Why make someone so beautiful, and kind and loving and just have her here for only 24 years? Why take away a blessing? Why is it that good people always seem to be taken from us first."

I found reassurance in the belief that Lisa's life, although short, had not been in vain. Even a short life has meaning.

Lisa had been a blessing to us all. She was a gift for the family and, when I think about it, what I had with my little sister for 24 years most people never have in an entire lifetime. I started to feel really lucky and grateful that I had shared a life with Lisa, that I was part of her journey, and I couldn't help but feel special that I could call this wonderful person my sister.

Lisa had been brought into this world under stressful circumstances and into a family of strong personalities. She showed so many people there was good in the world, even if it was only on a small scale, and she touched so many lives. She left something lasting for us to help us heal. And something I could share with others through my writing.

Looking back over Lisa's past, it was evident that, even from a young age, she was special. I very clearly remember the day Lisa came into the world. I was five years old when my mother was pregnant with Lisa and, while I may have been young, I remember some of the days around her pregnancy as if it was only yesterday.

I remember the day Mammy must have only had a few weeks left to go, possibly the month of March, as Lisa was born in April. Mammy was resting in her room and, of course, as clingy as ever as a child, I rarely gave her breathing space. I went upstairs and I remember asking Mammy what she thought the baby was going to be. Boy or Girl?

She told me it would be a girl.

I asked her what she would name the baby and she told me that there was only one name it could be, and that was Lisa Bernadette – Bernadette was my mother's name. Years later, I asked Mammy why she had been so certain of the name Lisa, so adamant. Mam said she loved the meaning of the name – Lisa means Oath of God. I suppose, looking back, my mother must have known how special Lisa would turn out to be and how Lisa, throughout her short life, would be so close to God.

Lisa was my mother's last child and they shared a very special bond, particularly because it was touch and go for both of them during the birth. There had been complications and my mother had been warned after giving birth to Lisa that she should not have any more children as it would risk her and any future baby's life.

So, Lisa and Mammy, from day one, had been through a lot and always shared something special. There was this running joke in our family that whatever fell out of Mammy's mouth fell into Lisa's. They were inseparable.

I remember the day Mammy came home with Lisa. I was outside playing rounders with Jane, Catherine and my friends when the car pulled up with Mammy and Lisa in it.

I was so excited that Mammy was home and, of course, to meet my little sister for the first time. I raced into the house after Mammy and there, in her arms, was the cutest little girl I had ever laid eyes on. I loved dolls and, to me, I suppose Lisa was now my little living doll. Lisa was a big baby, she was much bigger than the rest of us at almost nine pounds and she had these chubby cheeks and birdie lips.

I remember being allowed to hold her, with some help. I doted on her. Finally, I had a little sister. Up until then, I had attempted to fuss over my brother Michael and make him wear dresses and do his hair – well, I tried in vain.

Lisa, even from an early age, possessed an innate kindness like our mother. She was always a very sensitive and gentle child and, even in primary school, was eager to be of help to anyone who needed it. Ms Queally, her fifth class primary school teacher, went out of her way to inform Mammy that Lisa was a kind-hearted girl.

Ms Queally was actively involved in helping sick children and bringing them to Lourdes as part of a healing group. Each year, she would travel there to do her part with the sick children. When Lisa reached fifth class, Ms Queally asked Lisa to travel to Lourdes with her and help out for the week. She felt it was something Lisa would grow from and that the experience would further enhance the kindness that was already within her.

Of course, everyone in the family was delighted that Lisa was asked. She was so excited about that journey. She may only have been turning 12, but she was already a very spiritual child.

I recall the trip was during the Easter Holidays. I remember the morning Lisa was leaving for Lourdes and how excited she was. While she had dreadful travel sickness nothing could dampen her spirits. She loved that she would be visiting Lourdes and meeting new friends. We all missed her that week and the house was certainly a lot quieter without her in it.

When she returned home she was like a new girl. She was even more radiant than ever and was full of happy stories and she had lots of presents for all of us. She bought us these beautiful, colourful bracelets and other thoughtful gifts. She recounted that her favourite part of the visit was bathing in the holy water and the amazing, peaceful feeling she experienced afterwards. This was something Lisa would always refer to later in her teens and, even up until she died, she would reflect on how she felt something lift inside of her when she bathed in that water. She would always talk about that wonderful feeling. Lisa had made a lovely group of friends from the journey and would pray for the sick children she had travelled with.

As she grew older, her interest in sports became a passion and she was a keen swimmer, a good athlete and, as I've said, an excellent rounders player. Lisa excelled at any sport she took an interest in and loved taking part in competitions.

She was also very creative as a child and loved writing poetry. I remember how excited she had been in sixth class in school when she won a poetry competition. It was a big deal and we were all so proud of her. Her poem showed great depth for someone so young. It was fictional, but she wrote about loss and the impact the loss had had on the child left behind. While it may sound morbid, it wasn't really. It was like Lisa, even at that young age, could express what someone who had gone through loss would feel.

While she loved being involved in group events, she still had a slight shyness about her. She was never loud or brash, she was always softly spoken and a great listener. While she was growing up she didn't hang around with a big group but, instead, had two very close friends. However, as Lisa grew older, she broadened her social circle and really came out of her shell. She also became one of my best friends. That's what was so great. I could trust Lisa with anything, more than anyone, and I never feared that the trust would be broken as she had a loyalty unmatched by anyone.

When Lisa was 17 years old, she decided to become a hair stylist. It seemed like a perfect career choice for her, it would be another way for her to express her creativity. I had been living in Dublin, working in TV, for some time and had just moved jobs to work in a record company. I was thinking about getting my own place. I didn't like the idea of living alone and, at the same time, I had grown tired of house-sharing with strangers so, when Lisa asked me if she could move in with me, I was delighted. I loved her company and couldn't imagine a better person to live with. Of course Mammy wasn't totally ecstatic about it, as she loved having Lisa at home and enjoyed her company, but she never tried to stop her. She just told me to make sure I minded my little sister.

I put the plans in motion and went apartment hunting, while Lisa stayed at home until the time was right. I was so excited about her moving in with me.

At the time, Lisa was like a little country girl about to experience the big city. While she was fresh with innocence to start with, she soon found her feet. We moved into a small apartment on Rathgar Road. It suited both of us. I worked on Aylesbury Road and loved the long walks to work, whereas Lisa found a job in a hair salon in Rathmines, less than five minutes from our apartment.

Lisa was very nervous at first as it was her first proper job and, of course, it was a lot for her to get used to. She was living in a new city and about to experience new things. However, it wasn't long before she settled in and she really loved Dublin. She liked the girls she worked with, too, although most of them were a bit older than her. She later discovered that hair styling wasn't her calling but she made the most of her time in the salon and gave it her best shot.

I loved our girlie nights on Monday when we'd just chill after the weekend. Tuesday nights were pizza night and Wednesday night was laundry night. Thursday was girls' night out – we'd hook up with Jane, who only lived down the road, and the three of us would go out. On Fridays, when Lisa could, she'd go home to Mammy and stay for the weekend, and I'd go to Kilkenny to see my then partner. I was very uptight at that period in my life and pretty unhappy. I wasn't settled in my job and, I suppose, I wasn't settled in personal areas of my life either.

"Oh, you made things better for me by taking me to Dublin with you," Lisa would always tell me. She'd been bored and felt that she wasn't going anywhere in her hometown. In reality, though, it was Lisa who made things better for me. I had an unhealthy lifestyle, smoking 30 cigarettes a day, not eating properly, sometimes only eating one meal a day. Deep down, I was lonely. Having her around lifted my spirits, making my evenings happier, lighter times. Lisa helped me to heal myself and, soon, I was cooking for two, going for nice walks in the evening time and no longer feeling down. I also gave up smoking. Having such a positive influence around you soon changes you.

There are times, though, when I look back and wish I had made Lisa's time there more enjoyable, instead of being so stressed out. But then I remember all the laughs we had, too. Sometimes, we'd fall around laughing at our helplessness, like on our first night in the new place when we hadn't sorted out our beds and ended up asking the neighbours for help. Then there was the time we found a big spider in the bathroom and, though neither of us would kill it, neither of us could sleep knowing it was in there. So, once again, we needed to call upon our neighbours to help, this time to get rid of a creepy crawly.

While the apartment was nice, it was also old-style and almost antique-like. It was in a very well-to-do area and in a very secure building. However, Lisa felt creeped out by it and on the weekends she had to work she'd have to stay up in Dublin alone until I came back on the Sunday. She hated this. She'd no problem going out with the girls but she dreaded going back to sleep in the apartment alone.

I must admit, there were times things would move or we'd hear weird noises that we couldn't explain and, no matter how hard we tried, we just couldn't get that place warm. Lisa was so freaked out one night that, rather than sleep in the bed, she went and slept on the stairway that all the residents shared. I knew Lisa couldn't live like that, being so scared, so I made more of an effort to stay over at the weekends and at other times she would stay with Jane.

At this stage, Lisa didn't really express much of an interest in men. Whenever we would go out there would be a host of guys asking her for her number and trying to buy her drinks. She never really cared for it, and was always just about having fun.

One of the weekends, Lisa went home and that was the start of something new for her. She was going out with Catherine in Leighlinbridge. During the night Catherine introduced Lisa to someone she considered a friend. One of the nice guys in the area. He had been in a long-term relationship himself, engaged to one of the local girls from the area. Like Lisa, he was healing his wounds after a breakup and wasn't looking for a relationship, but they seemed to hit it off. Lisa kissed him that night but no plans were made to ever meet again. She wasn't interested in starting anything new and it seemed neither was he. It turned out, she said, he knew me from school, he had been a few years above me. His brother had been in my class for a few years until transition year. I asked her what he was like and she told me he was handsome, really friendly and easy going.

She told me his name was Ger O'Hara.

He was almost six years older than her but he was nice, Lisa insisted. I tried to place him. It took me a while and, when I did, I recalled he just seemed like one of those very quiet guys. I remembered a girl he had dated and knew they had been together for a few years but I said no more, as I knew nothing else about him.

Lisa never mentioned him again and it would be another two years before they would meet once more, in the very same place. It seemed that, no matter what, this dark force was going to find Lisa, one way or the other.

The months flew by in Dublin and, before we knew it, it was almost Christmas. We both had two weeks off work and Lisa was going home to Bagenalstown. I was going back to Kilkenny. However, that all changed on December 11, when Mammy died.

I'll never forget poor Lisa's face when I told her the news. She had just come back from the shop as I was sitting on the bed crying. Having to tell her Mammy was gone was devastating. Just hours before, we had both been excited and running around packing our bags, making phone calls and arranging our lift home.

It was a horrendous time for all of us but Lisa, although she was the youngest, showed amazing strength.

Christmas passed in a blur and Lisa and I returned to work later that January. At this point we both realised it was time for a change, we wanted out of Dublin, our hearts weren't in it any more. The need to be closer to loved ones grew stronger and, that March, I handed in my notice at work. A few weeks later, Lisa handed in hers and packed her bags and returned home.

CHAPTER

I had moved to Kilkenny and found a job in local radio as a sports producer and joined one of the newspapers as their fashion editor, while Lisa began taking an interest in modelling. I started to involve Lisa in my work and would have her model for the fashion shoots and shows I was involved in.

She loved it all, particularly the shows and meeting people. Soon, she was taking part in fashion shows and events separate to my work and having a ball.

Unable to find full-time work Lisa decided to broaden her knowledge and enrolled in a health and beauty therapy course in Kilkenny.

The course was fun, but also intensive and I quickly learned that beauty courses are very difficult. The amount of notes Lisa would bring home was unbelievable. The biology section of the course is similar to that for nursing so it wasn't all plain sailing for her. At times, she would get a little stressed out. Lisa's favourite part of the course was learning about the body, about massage and make-up, and I was her willing 'guinea pig' on more than one occasion. At this stage, Lisa was living with my father and brother,

Michael, in our home place.

Michael and Lisa were inseparable around that time and really became the best of friends. During her nine-month intensive course, Lisa and I got to spend a lot of time together, too.

I'd drag her along to fashion shows and events during the week and she'd come with me on nights out. On one of those nights out, she met a lovely guy and they started dating immediately. The relationship didn't last more than four months, as they were both young, but they ended it as friends.

Seeing him again, all those years later at Lisa's funeral, I just kept thinking, God, isn't it a pity they hadn't worked out as he was such a lovely guy and Lisa had really liked him.

Before her course ended, Lisa wanted to start dating again. One Sunday, after being out the night before with Catherine in Leighlinbridge, she called me. She sounded so happy and not at all like someone who'd been out the night before.

"I met him again!" she quickly told me

I was barely awake.

"Who, Robert?' I asked.

"No!" she replied. "Don't you remember, about two years ago, the guy I met from Fenagh, the one I really liked? He knows you. Ger O'Hara is his name," continued Lisa, full of happiness and excitement. "Well, we met last night and we chatted, had a few drinks, and I had a great laugh with him. Catherine was there and Martin [Catherine's partner], and all their mutual friends."

I could almost see Lisa glowing down the phone.

I asked her were they already a couple. "No, we're just going to hang out for a while, and take it from there."

Of course, like any sister, I was happy for Lisa. She reminded me he was six years older than her but this didn't bother me, in fact, I thought it was a good thing as he would be mature and less likely to mess Lisa around, or so I thought.

When Lisa came back to stay with me the following week for her beauty course, she was a young woman in love. She was really happy and kept telling me how much she liked him. She said he was very smart and nice and quiet, and he worked in scaffolding. He had also finally moved on from his last relationship and was ready to settle.

At first, I thought, Settle? That's moving a bit fast.

But Lisa didn't seem concerned and was content to have found, in her words, "a nice guy".

The first time I met Ger O'Hara with Lisa had been in the pub in Leighlinbridge and I had dropped him home to Fenagh afterwards. I'd felt uncomfortable with him beside me in the passenger seat but hadn't said anything about it to Lisa. I suppose it hadn't really been a proper meeting anyway. When I met him again with Lisa, it was at our home place. They had been seeing each other for only a few months at this point but, already, the relationship was moving very fast. If it's right, it's right, I thought.

I remember walking into the house and he was sitting there. He said a faint, "Hello," and I thought he seemed very shy so I didn't push any conversation out of him that time, as I didn't want to highlight his shyness or make him uncomfortable.

He seemed fine chatting to my father. Our fathers had been in school together as they had grown up in the same place.

"He seems like a nice chap," my father said to me after he left. "His father is a very nice man. Quiet man, too, they're all very quiet in that family."

I thought, while he may be quiet, he and Lisa weren't shy about showing their affection for one another.

At this stage in the relationship they were going out every weekend, like any young couple. But I rarely got to see Lisa as I was socialising in Kilkenny and she was now fitting right in at home in Leighlinbridge, with his friends and Catherine. Lisa was very content around that time and had become more confident.

She stopped modelling in the fashion shoots and told me she no longer wanted to do them, as she was very happy just as things were. I didn't push her.

She was also coming towards the end of her course and I insisted she come on a girls' holiday with me, as my treat. As it happened, unbeknownst to me, O'Hara and a friend had already booked a holiday at the same time. Initially, Lisa had been reluctant to go away and leave him but, when she realised we would all be away at the same time, she was up for it.

I remember that day though. We were at our home place in Carlow where I had filled Lisa in on the holiday plans. She and O'Hara walked out to the garden to wait for his mother who was going to come and collect him because he had no car at the time.

They were having a tiff, not a fight or anything but things weren't one hunderd per cent, I could tell by their body language and their expressions. I never found out what it was about. After Ger's mother had collected him, Lisa came back inside looking flustered so I asked Lisa if she was alright. She reassured me that everything was fine and skipped over the subject, saying she was looking forward to getting away.

After the holidays, when they had broken up for that short time, Lisa spent more time with me. She started to come down to Kilkenny again and even took part in a few more fashion shows. However, after a night out in Leighlinbridge, they met again and he asked Lisa back. Their relationship started again.

Lisa was happy with this and I didn't mind, as long as she was happy. I was concerned by what happened while we were on holiday but I had already voiced that with Lisa and couldn't say much more on the subject.

During this time, Lisa found a job with my sister, Catherine, in the retirement home in Leighlinbridge. Lisa would say it was hard work but very rewarding and I remember telling her how much I'd love someone like her minding me when I was older!

She was still living at home but O'Hara was spending a lot of time there with her. She would get the bus into work in the morning, or a taxi as it was only a short drive, and his mother would collect him on days he stayed over with Lisa.

After months of hard work, Lisa wanted to find another job and meet more people. She read an advertisement looking for people for the new Argos store that was about to open in Carlow and Lisa was determined to get a job there. After sending in her CV and undergoing a successful interview she was offered a position. She was, at the time, concerned about the tills and the maths side of it – maths is not a strong point in our family. As it turned out, O'Hara was a great help in this regard and taught her new ways of grasping maths. In her words, he was a great help to her.

As she was going to be working in Carlow and they were now getting serious, they decided to officially move in together. She joked that she would get rid of the mammy's boy in him and teach him to be more independent. At this stage, Lisa had become close to his family as well. She told me she really liked his mother, that she was a lovely woman and really nice to talk to. His little sister was also someone Lisa was very fond of and I know, to this day, that Lisa would hate any hardship coming their way.

It wasn't long before Lisa and O'Hara were house hunting together and they eventually found a place in Carlow but they didn't stay in it for long.

Lisa had very strange experiences while living there. I never had a chance to visit this first place but, from what I gather, Lisa was pretty spooked. She kept on finding unusual letters around the place. They didn't really make sense to her. Unfortunately, I never got to see them but I'm told they were almost like suicide letters, or else letters written by a very depressed person, and she found them in the room she and O'Hara shared. She told Michael and his partner, Margaret, about them and described how odd the letters were. Lisa was freaked out and decided to throw them away. As a result of all this, it wasn't too long before they were moving to a better and more homely place in Carlow.

When they moved into their second place, I did get to visit. I called over one day. It was a nice house so Lisa gave me the tour while Ger was downstairs doing a crossword.

"He loves doing them," she told me. "He's well able to get them and is really smart."

She was always complimenting him.

He was in good enough form that day and lent me one of his CDs. I had recently come out of a long relationship and he was being nice to me. I had just moved back in with my father and was a bit all over the place, still trying to find my feet. Lisa, as usual, was very kind and was making sure I was alright. I had a cup of tea and chatted to Lisa while he did his crossword. I could see she was happy in the house. She told me about her new job and how lovely everyone was. She loved that they were all new in the job together, how they were all learning at the same time.

I left a very content Lisa that day and thought they seemed nice and settled. However, it wasn't long before he lost his job, like so many others in the construction business, and Lisa became the main bread-winner. Unfortunatley, this meant they could no longer afford to stay in that house and had to begin searching for somewhere smaller and more affordable. They soon found another place in Carlow and things seem to settle again. At this stage, Lisa was already speaking about their future together and even having children one day. "I'll go out and do the work," she told me, "and leave him at home being the child minder."

I still couldn't figure him out but he didn't unnerve me either at that stage. I was in a new relationship – with Stephen – and was so caught up in that that I didn't notice much else around me. I had moved out of my father's and into a small apartment in Kilkenny.

I had been telling Lisa about Stephen and how much I liked him and that I couldn't wait for them to meet. I had even suggested we go away on a couples' holiday together at some point but O'Hara was having none of it. Lisa would have welcomed the idea but she told me he wanted their first break to just be the two of them. I could understand that.

Lisa couldn't wait for their first holiday together to Bulgaria. They'd booked it in the travel agent in Bagenalstown. Afterwards, I saw their holiday photos and Lisa looked happy in them, it seemed like they had had fun. She said they hadn't ventured too far and had spent most of their time in the resort.

Things seemed to tick along nicely for them and I believe he found work here and there, nothing permanent but a few casual jobs. Before I knew it, though, he and Lisa were moving out of their place in Carlow.

It was getting close to winter and they found the rented house was very cold and costly to heat so, once again, they were up and moving. It didn't really faze Lisa too much. She was very laid back about things and she was happy as long as they were together. Their budget didn't allow them to rent another place of their own, so they found themselves having to move in with my father. While Lisa didn't mind at first, it wasn't exactly in her plans.

There was more big news when O'Hara proposed to Lisa. It wasn't a big romantic proposal, but Lisa was very happy and they chose the ring together. They hadn't made any definite plans for a wedding but they seemed happy to be engaged.

CHAPTER 9

It wasn't long after they became engaged that Lisa and O'Hara decided they needed their own place. They had worked out their budget and, once again, they moved back into Carlow. This would be the last place they would live together.

They found a nice three-bedroom house and they got themselves a dog. I can't remember his name but he was massive. Lisa rescued him from the pound and would say he must have been ill treated because he was very hyper – even crazy – but she loved him regardless and said she wanted to help him.

They moved into their home at the end of November, 2007, and were excited about making it theirs. I didn't have a chance to see it until January, 2008, because Lisa had spent Christmas with the O'Hara's and I didn't see her. Steve, who had by now become an important part of my life, was making the journey with me to Carlow to wish them a Happy Christmas and drop off gifts. Lisa still had her decorations and Christmas tree up.

I think it was at this time that I first started to notice something was not right with Ger O'Hara.

While I always knew he was quiet and didn't have much conversation in him, this time it was different, and it worried me. As we were walking into the house, Lisa told me that he was on these tablets for giving up smoking and how proud she was of him, as he was such a heavy smoker.

So, I wondered was this the reason he was more stand-offish than normal. When Steve and I went into the house, though, I couldn't help but notice his body language and stance, that spoke louder than his few words, he seemed to be letting us know that he was not happy we had called over.

He barely uttered a hello.

Steve and I noticed this immediately and we both knew that it was only Lisa who wanted us there, it was that obvious. Lisa brought us into the kitchen and offered us tea. We sat at the table. It was a six-seated table and very big. Lisa sat opposite me, full of smiles, while Steve was beside me and Ger sat down at the opposite end, at the very top of the table, rather than sit beside Lisa or face Steve. He was making it obvious he wanted as much distance between us and him as possible.

That wasn't all. He had a piece of plastic in his hand and he sat there, flicking it. At first, I thought it was some sort of cigarette substitute, but he was holding it between his thumb and index finger and flicking it towards us. It looked to me as if he was flicking it at us, as if to say 'get out'. Lisa, of course, was so full of chat that you couldn't really notice the silence at the other end of the table. I soon gave up trying to include him in conversation, but Steve tried. And he just mumbled back, a yes, or a no.

Not once did O'Hara initiate a conversation. We stayed there for over an hour and, while it was great to see Lisa, we felt very uncomfortable. He didn't smile once, not until we said we were leaving and, at that, it was more like a smirk than a nice smile.

Steve decided to go out ahead and get the car warm for me. O'Hara stayed in the kitchen, he didn't even walk us out. I pulled

Lisa aside on the way out.

"Lisa, that was really weird and uncomfortable," I whispered to her. "With him in there! He didn't speak a word!"

Lisa was used to me being upfront and saying it as it was. She laughed.

"Ah, that's just him."

"No, Lisa!" I replied. "That was odd, he didn't even speak to us. I felt very uneasy in there with him. And what was he doing flicking that piece of plastic towards us?"

"Ah no, he's grand," Lisa repeated.

I warned her that, next time, he needed to say a few words. She continued to smile. She said she was so used to his behaviour she couldn't see anything wrong in it. When we got into the car Steve also had something to say about what had just happened, which was unusual for Steve.

"I'm not trying to give out or that but did you feel weird in there, with him not saying anything to us?'

I was relieved the strangeness of what had just occured wasn't in my head. I admitted to Steve that I was worried. I told him that I wanted to take Lisa with me. And I wondered if O'Hara also sat there in silence when there were just the two of them in the house. To me, he looked like someone on the edge, which added to my worry. Never before, had I imagined that he would hurt Lisa and, while I didn't voice that direct concern at the time, looking back I wonder if that was my uneasy feeling. Could I, subconsciously, see that he was capable of hitting Lisa? I just wish I had been more tuned in. I wish I hadn't accepted his behaviour. I did, however, call Lisa the next day and I asked if everything was alright between them. I told her I was worried, I told her that he seemed very on edge. Lisa just put it down to him being off the cigarettes. She also said that one of the side-effects of the tablets was nausea and he felt like he needed to vomit all the time. Lisa said he'd just started the medication the day before we called and wasn't in the best of form, between quitting and having to deal with the sickness. I actually felt a bit guilty when I heard Lisa's explanation. Was I wrong to have judged him so harshly? I was also relieved that I had nothing to worry about after all.

"Right!" I said to Lisa, "In a few weeks, no excuses, the two of ye come down to myself and Steve for the night and we will have a few drinks in my place."

I told her not to worry about the cost. I knew they were minding their money. I told her we would pay for the drinks. "Then we'll hit town." I told her. Lisa knew I wouldn't give up and agreed. As I had given them a few weeks' notice I knew they couldn't back out. In the past, I wouldn't have thought of doing that, but things had changed. I felt he would just have come up with some excuse if I hadn't been prepared.

Leading up to the evening out, I made sure to text Lisa, telling her that there was no backing out. "Ye are coming down to us ... and I can't wait," I informed her. I began to get very excited about our night out together. It had been way too long since we had had a proper night out so, as my treat, I booked Lisa in for a full body tan and treatment, to get our girlie preparations off to a good start. The following evening she and Ger took the train down, I had offered to collect them but they said they wanted to get the train.

This time, when they arrived, O'Hara, while slightly awkward was more chatty and when Steve gave him a few drinks he seemed to loosen up and didn't seem at all uncomfortable. Plus, he was back on the cigarettes and there were now no excuses for his moods. While he still couldn't really look me in the eye, he smiled a lot, and he would laugh at whatever Steve said.

Lisa and I got ready in the bedroom, doing our makeup and the usual bits of preening, and then we joined the lads. Steve, of course, was doing most of the talking but O'Hara seemed interested and was in good form. When we got to the pub later, it wasn't long before some of Steve's friends were asking who Lisa was. One or two strangers were trying to get her attention, too. Lisa, as always, was oblivious to this or paid no attention. Steve asked O'Hara did he not get bothered that Lisa got such attention and asked if he ever got jealous He replied that he didn't mind. He said he never got jealous or was ever bothered by it. To me, he seemed to enjoy it and take some satisfaction from any attention Lisa was given. Then again, Lisa would never flirt so he probably felt secure with her. That night they seemed very comfortable with each other, like it didn't matter who else was around. They were just chatting to each other and happy in each other's company.

It was good to see them so happy that night, even if he did still seem awkward with me. But what I had begun to notice was that, despite saying he wasn't jealous, he was definitely more possessive than before. This side of his personality was becoming more and more evident during that year.

Previously, I could arrange to see Lisa whenever I wanted and we would do things together, just the two of us. Now, I had begun to noticed that at any social event we atttended he wouldn't leave her side. It was as if he was stuck to her.

At my nephew Justin's confirmation Jane noticed something wasn't fully right. She hadn't seen Lisa in a few weeks and they couldn't get a seat together in the church because it was packed. Jane had really being missing Lisa and had not heard from her in a while so, when she looked over at him and Lisa, walking outside the church, Jane waved but Lisa looked away.

Jane thought she had done something wrong and, when we got to the restaurant, she asked Lisa why she hadn't greeted her when they came out of the church. Lisa, for some reason, had thought Jane wasn't talking to her either and explained that that was why she didn't give her a big hello.

In fact, Lisa hadn't given me a big hello either, which was out of character for her. At this stage Lisa started to get upset and, naturally, we all soothed her and wondered what had brought it all on. Looking back, it wasn't anything that Jane had said that had caused those tears, it was what was being said by Ger. It was obvious that he had been putting thoughts into her head, suggesting that she and her family were falling out. Everything was soon alright again and Jane and Lisa hugged and had a great chat.

Then Jane sat down beside O'Hara and said, "Oh, I hope you're okay, I didn't mean for Lisa to be upset." Jane adored Lisa, and Lisa adored Jane, and ordinarily we could just ask each other any question. That day, it seemed Lisa was feeling extra sensitive, something deeper was going on.

Jane had always thought O'Hara was a nice, quiet fella because he was very good at playing that role when she was around. His reply left her shocked and upset. He said, "I don't give a fuck what you say, it doesn't bother me."

His true personality was coming out. Beneath that false smile and quietness was someone who was incapable of caring. I believe his inability to care or show proper love was bringing Lisa down, too. She was not as bubbly as her old self. While she was just as kind and caring as ever, his lack of connection was taking a heavy toll on her.

Jane was disgusted, as was I when I heard what he had said. He had uttered the words with total conviction.

We could all see now that he was odd and ignorant but none of us could ever have seen what he was capable of. How could we?

If I hadn't liked him before, I certainly didn't after the confirmation. But Lisa was devoted to him and there was nothing we could say. There was no sign that he was physically hurting Lisa and, in my heart, I knew that if he had been Lisa would have told me. She may have loved him but that was one thing Lisa would never ever have put up with, and she would have told me if that had happened. So, while we didn't like him, there was no way we could interfere.

A few weeks after Justin's confirmation Lisa called me and said she was thinking of going up to see Jane in Dublin. I was delighted because, even after Lisa and I had left Dublin, we would occasionally arrange a trip to the city where the three of us would have a lovely meal and go out afterwards. I thought Lisa was planning this kind of trip again.

"Brilliant!" I said, "We'll get the train up, or I'll drive, it'll be like old times."

"No," Lisa said. "I'm only going to go up for the day because Ger wants to come too."

This surprised me. Surely he could see we were planning a girls' night out? He would have known how much we liked those times together.

"Why does he have to come up?" I asked. "Surely we can have our girls' night. He can survive without you for one night."

Lisa sounded wary. She said the two of them wanted to drive up and down. I asked her to tell him she was having a girls' night but Lisa wasn't too convinced about that. I felt by her tone that she was under pressure, so I said, "Okay, Li, you go ahead. At least you're getting to go up and visit Jane, she'll be delighted."

Lisa, I could tell, was very relieved but I could also tell she was nostalgic for those days we'd had, too.

Towards the end of the conversation, I realised he was sitting there, right next to her the whole time we'd been talking, listening to every word. In fact, I heard him as he whispered something faintly to her.

"Oh, is he listening in to our conversation?" I asked jokingly. I said it lightly, but I knew full well he was. I said hello to him, and he said hello back, which confirmed for me he'd been listening all along.

Lisa and O'Hara visited Jane a few days later and the girls had a lovely day together.

Jane took them to a park and Ger played with Jane's son while Lisa and she chatted. Some time later, Jane would tell me that she had felt Lisa was very close to her that day, walking beside her very closely, as if she needed the comfort.

Jane didn't really chat to Ger, and she said he only ever stared over at them, always keeping one eye on them.

When the time came for them to go, Jane found it odd that he was unable to speak up. He said, barely audibly, under his breath, "We may go now."

Jane wasn't sure at first if she had heard him clearly, but when Lisa replied that they would go in a while he didn't look too impressed at being second-guessed. But he said nothing more in front of Jane.

I was very annoyed at the way O'Hara was getting in the way of my relationship with Lisa. I didn't like that he was preventing us from getting together and doing simple sisterly stuff. At this point, they stopped going out socially.

Their excuse was always that they were saving money for the wedding but we later learned that they hadn't saved anything. He knew that the less time they spent out and about, the less time Lisa spent with those who loved her.

It was 2008, and that July 12, it was Christopher's birthday and when I discovered that Lisa wasn't turning up for the party I knew for sure that he was intent on keeping her to himself. He refused to give her a lift to the party. I rang Lisa and asked where she was. She said he was watching a football game on TV and wouldn't give her a lift so I had Michael go and collect Lisa and bring her to the party.

She was hesitant at first and I had to remind her it was Christopher's birthday, that it was important that she be there. I told her she had her lift.

O'Hara hadn't expected one of us to drive over and collect her but now there was nothing he could do about it. Of course, he didn't come with her that day. I suppose he couldn't, after making his excuse about watching some game, but at least we got her there.

She seemed more relaxed when he wasn't with her. I noticed that a lot in the last year, that when he wasn't around, Lisa was less on guard, more herself and more carefree. I knew how happy she was to be part of the birthday celebrations that July, and thrilled to be seeing her family. While she was there, he must have texted her several times because any time her phone beeped it was him and, several times, Lisa would just roll her eyes as if to say, Why is he texting me ... sure I'll see him soon enough?

We all sang happy birthday to Chris, gave him our gifts and, before long, we were all saying our goodbyes and heading home. I asked Lisa did she want to go down the road with me for a coffee and a chat before she headed off, and I knew she wanted to, but she said she couldn't.

He had already cooked her dinner and was expecting her home.

I gave her a hug goodbye and said I'd see her at the next family event. We both smiled, because that's how it was beginning to play out. We were only getting to spend time with one another at family get-togethers.

CHAPTER 10

It was mid-September and I had just come back home from a holiday but, despite the break, I was still feeling out of sorts. I was convinced that O'Hara was tyring to prevent Lisa and me from getting together.

I decided to call Lisa. I told her that I wasn't feeling myself at all and asked if I could call to see her that weekend, so we agreed to meet on the Sunday.

By the Tuesday, I was very glad that I had organised our meeting as I knew if anyone could make me feel centred, or just give me that peaceful feeling, it was Lisa.

It turned out Steve had to work that weekend and, at the time, we only had the one car as mine was giving me trouble. So, my brother Michael, as accommodating as always, said he would collect me from Kilkenny and drop me off at Lisa's, and bring me back home that evening.

The weekend couldn't come fast enough. Michael collected me at about 11.30am and we drove up to Leighlin. He still hadn't been in Lisa's new place but he knew where it was.

"They mustn't be there, Angela," he said, as we drove down the street.

"Why not?" I asked.

"Cos his car's not there ... and these days you won't see Lisa without him."

I told Michael it was grand, that Lisa knew I was coming round and we'd arranged a girls' day. I told Michael she wouldn't let me down but he wasn't so sure. Anyway, I got out of the car and knocked on the door.

A beautiful, beaming Lisa answered, delighted I was there. She waved at Michael, who said he'd leave us to it and call in later. I went inside the house and she asked if I'd like the tour. It was an older house, nice, but still very old. To the right as we entered was a small sitting room where Lisa had already put her books up on the shelf and her lovely colourful, flowery pictures on the walls. She showed me the downstairs bedroom which had a single bed, already dressed for guests or for me whenever I wished to sleep over. We then made our way upstairs where we had a look at the bathroom where all of Lisa's toiletries were neatly stacked. There was a big mirror on the wall, almost the size of the wall itself, and it was hanging right in front of the toilet. It was covered with a sheet. I asked her why she had covered it and she laughed, saying neither of them wanted to be staring at themselves every time they were in the bathroom. She didn't like its size either, which we agreed about.

We entered the bedroom. She had it nicely made up and, on her locker, there were a few pieces of jewellery and a money box filled with change that she was trying to save.

I asked her was she not a little creeped out there, as it was an old house – I'm a big coward and I told her that I would be. She laughed, and that was when she first told me, "Sure why would I ... I'm never alone ... sure isn't he here minding me."

She quickly insisted that we move on to see the outside. "Oh, you have to come out to the back garden, it's massive, and Ger spent all day yesterday mowing the lawn, he's done a great job."

The garden was a lovely size. Lisa sat on the wall and I stood in front of her. It was a beautiful warm, sunny, Sunday afternoon and it was so peaceful and calm. Lisa talked about how she could really see her children and mine running around the garden some day. I agreed, it was safe and enclosed with plenty of space to run around in. We both smiled at our thoughts.

"You really want that, don't you?" I said.

"Angela, don't get me wrong, there's loads I want to do but, my biggest dream is to settle down, have children and get married. To me that's the most important thing, nothing would beat that."

I told her I wanted that too, just not now, maybe down the road. She laughed again and said I was gas. "You're almost six years older than me," she added, "but in a way I should be living your life and you living mine." My fiancé was seven years younger than me, and closer to Lisa's age, while O'Hara was closer to my age.

Steve and I went on holidays twice a year and enjoyed going out most weekends, living it up. While Lisa was staying in with her feet up and eating take-aways at the weekends. All of which she thoroughly enjoyed, she said, and we laughed about this. But I did think even then that Lisa should be doing more instead of stressing so much about bills and settling down so soon.

We soon got down to some serious chat and I told her how Steve's work contract would end the following March and he didn't know what he was going to do then. I explained that we'd be grand on my wage, for a while anyway and, besides, Steve was so versatile that he'd find a job somewhere.

Lisa wasn't so sure.

"Oh, Angela, you'll feel a lot of pressure," she told me. "You'll be the one who'll have all the responsibility, covering most of the bills, trying to get more hours in work. And you'll feel bad that he's at home all day, on his own, and bored. It can drain you," she said.

I'd never heard Lisa speak like that before. I knew she was right, in a way, and that it was a lot of pressure with only one wage. She said that she'd bought things for him, like an Xbox, so that he could invite his friends who weren't working over during the day.

"At least he has company and people to chat to," she added.

We went into the sitting room. I was looking at the books on dreams that Lisa had. I told her I'd been really disturbed by my dreams lately, and that it was as if I were being haunted, it felt so unsettling because the dreams seemed so real.

I also told her that I'd experienced a vision of a woman. She asked if my visions were actually Mammy but I told her they weren't, that the spirit I'd seen seemed to be a young woman with long, flowy hair. I was unable to get a clear look at her features.

She told me about the dreams she'd had since moving into the house. She described waking up in the middle of the night because she was laughing so hard. She wondered what I thought this meant.

"It must be because I'm just so happy," she added.

It was then that she had informed me that she felt that Mammy was with her since she moved into the house and believed that she had appeared to her. She felt it was very real and wasn't particularly frightened by the experience. I'd told her she had probably been a little stressed with all the moving and I said that Mammy was here to help her to settle in. That's truly what I believed.

I needed Lisa to know how unsure I had been feeling, that somehow I felt out of sync, and being with her had really lifted me out of it. Just being by her side and talking had been a huge help and I wanted her to know. She came over and hugged me and said the usual, lovely reassuring things a sister says.

I suggested it would be nice to call up the road to see Catherine and the family. As we walked, I felt she was very content, there was a maturity in her that I hadn't seen before. I could really see my little sister was no longer a little girl, but a strong, confident woman. We linked arms and called in to see the boys. They were happy to see us and we played with Nathan, Catherine's little boy, for about half an hour. Lisa then suggested we go back to her house for tea.

We made our way down the street.

"Oh, I hope he's here!" Lisa exclaimed.

I was surprised.

"Why?" I asked. I was so enjoying our time together.

"Oh, no, not because of that, I don't have a house key."

I was more surprised.

"Why don't you have a key? If he's gone off and you leave the house, does that mean that you're out on your own for however long it takes for him to get back?"

"Yeah ... that's it," she admitted.

I asked Lisa why they didn't have two sets of keys. Why should he have the comfort of the car and the house keys? But, before I got to vent any further, I saw the car was there. As we got closer I could see the curtain moving and, just before Lisa knocked, he opened the door. There was a bare "hello" to me.

"Your place is lovely," I told him. "I see ye have my bedroom made up and all for my visits." I was joking with him. He smiled.

"Yeah," he replied.

Lisa and I sat down, Lisa on the couch under the window and me on the armchair. I was making general chat with Lisa when he came into the room. He sat down on the couch beside Lisa, but I sensed that there was a distance between them.

He had a sandwich on a small plate. He had been out playing a soccer match so I asked how he had got on

"Grand," he answered.

"Did you score a goal?" I went on.

"Nope."

And that was it it.

Just then, I suddenly realised my own house keys were missing so I said I must have left them upstairs. Suddenly, O'Hara slammed down his plate and got up, as if to go and get my keys. It was very strange, I had never really seen a reaction out of him before, but this time he was extremely tense.

"Ger, please sit down, eat your snack." I said. "I didn't mean for you to get my keys for me."

I was baffled as to why he thought I did. He said nothing, looked at me and sat back down again and continued eating. As it turned out, I found the keys on the chair I had being sitting on.

Michael soon came and O'Hara said hello to him before announcing he was going out to the back garden to have a cigarette. Michael, Lisa and I stayed inside and chatted about Michael's beautiful identical twin girls. Lisa was Godmother to one of them.

Eventually, O'Hara came back into the sitting room. As we got up to leave, Lisa walked us out and gave us both a hug and kiss goodbye, and I told her I'd call or text her during the week. I told her I'd be up to visit again soon.

I said goodbye to O'Hara and told him again that I was happy they had their own place and that Lisa had been singing his praises about the gardening. He just smiled. That night, after my visit with Lisa, I slept soundly and there was no bad dream.

On Monday night the dreams started all over again. I was very jumpy and, by Wednesday evening, I felt overwhelmed by death. I remember texting my cousin, Laura, and she was concerned by the tone of my message. I told her I was seeing and feeling things around me and couldn't get rid of the sense that something bad was about to happen. I told Steve I wasn't going to bed on Wednesday night and he asked why. I told him, frankly, that I thought I was going to die, that I had a strong feeling of death. I told him that I was sure this was my last night.

He was his usual calm self and told me that wasn't going to happen, that there was nothing wrong with me. Although I knew that, it felt to me that my time was up. He tried to reassure and soothe me and, in the end, I agreed to go to the bedroom only if I could leave the TV on and watch all night.

Poor Steve fell asleep not too long after.

I stayed awake, fighting sleep as best I could. I eventually succumbed to the tiredness in the early hours and woke up surprised, and relieved, that it had all just been a bad feeling and that I was still alive.

That Thursday, I wasn't working so I kept myself busy and made plans for my cousin, Teresa's, visit towards the end of that year. I texted Jane, Catherine and Lisa, and said we should all have a girls' night when she's home. That night I slept quite well. I was looking forward to our dinner plans with Steve's sister, Therese, and her husband, Owen on Friday night.

At dinner, I chatted to Therese, who is very easy-going, about my awful night on Wednesday and how convinced I was of my impending death. She thought it was strange to be feeling that way and wondered what could cause such a feeling. In spite of that, we had a lovely night with them and I drank a few glasses of wine which helped me to sleep when I got home.

On Saturday, Steve and I had plans to meet up with all his friends and their girlfriends, as we would normally do at the weekend. It started as another good day – Lisa texted and told me she was going out to Leighlin that night with Catherine and asked what my plans were and did I want to call up, too. She didn't mind when I told her we were going out and suggested we organise a night out together very soon. I told her I loved her and to enjoy her night out, I told her I would see her very soon.

My mood slowly changed as the evening progressed and, finally, I said to Steve that I wasn't feeling up to going out. I felt I just wasn't in the mood and asked if he'd mind if we stayed in. At first, he wondered what had brought about my change of mind but I didn't know, I just knew that I didn't feel up to going out and wanted to go to bed early instead. That was no problem for Steve. He went off and had a shower.

While he was in the shower, I sat on a small chair in the bedroom and there, once again in front of me, I could see the outline of a young woman.

I got such a fright.

This time, she was much clearer than before and I ran into the bathroom and didn't leave until Steve was ready to come out. He had become used to my behaviour and didn't doubt any of it for a second. He knew it wasn't something I would make up. It was something that was scary and unsettling for me and I didn't know why it was happening.

We decided we'd blank it out and watch the 'X Factor' in bed. I must have been asleep by 10.30 that night. I slept right through and, when the phone call came that Sunday morning, something clicked in my head.

It was like all the worry, the anxiety and the unsettled feelings seemed to connect to what I was about to find out.

CHAPTER 11

I truly believed I'd never recover from that day. I didn't believe it would be possible. But, life has a funny way of changing things. I found there were so many ways of healing being presented to me that, as time went on, I began to make progress.

I was getting there.

There were times, though, when I found myself looking back to when my mother had died and the last day I hugged her goodbye. I struggled when I remembered the fear I had felt then.

My God! I had thought at that moment. This is the last time ... please God, don't let my mother die!

I had told my partner at that time of my experience and my feelings, the certainty I felt that our kiss and hug goodbye would be our last.

And I was right.

In the weeks before Lisa died, those same feelings were even stronger than they had been when I hugged Mammy for the last time. But, I just couldn't recognise them, or fully understand what they meant, until that morning when the phone rang. Then, everything, tragically, fell into place.

When my mother died, I hadn't experienced any feelings of guilt. There were no What ifs?

My mother and I never had an argument. If we did, I certainly couldn't remember it. I felt she always knew I loved her and, even that last day together, we felt extremely close. She was an amazing mother and I will always miss her and mourn her passing at such a young age. I will always live with a sadness about her passing and there will always be times that I just want to call her up, ask her advice and opinions even though I know I can't do that.

However, after Lisa's death, especially in that first year, I experienced huge waves of guilt. I was so sorry that I hadn't or couldn't see what was happening, that I couldn't protect my little sister. Of course, I know it wasn't my fault that she died nor anyone else's, only his. But, at the same time, it seemed utterly impossible to come to terms with what had occurred.

I was left with so many things I wanted to discuss with Lisa, none of them seem that major but, still, they are little things that are important to me.

I would like to believe people are capable of change and are willing to do their best but, even now, I still get flashbacks of his admission that he, "always knew some day I would do something bad," in the words he wrote in the letter to the Gardai. The fact that he admitted to what he felt he was capable of doing but didn't seek help. Even if he does seek help in prison, for me O'Hara is incapable of truly letting go of those 'urges', as he called them.

However, I need to remind myself that this is part of the reason I'm writing Lisa's story. To let people in on this amazing young woman's life and to allow people to see the impact that evil actions have on other lives. To keep it known that this man is a murderer.

In the months after Lisa's death, I found that some of my strange experiences were becoming overpowering. I started to have very clear and interesting dreams. The dreams were more like little movies of other people's lives, snippets of typical day-to-day things that, at the time, seemed unimportant to me but when I'd mention them to the people who were the subject of my dreams they would tell me how very significant and accurate they were.

My dreams were premonitions.

I foresaw pregnancies and, soon after, I'd learn that the person was pregnant. I saw emotional struggles in the lives of my friends and, some days later, I would discover that I had been given a clear insight into what was actually happening in their lives. A few friends were shocked, and a little disturbed, by what I told them.

So, I stopped telling people about my dreams.

Around three months after the predictive dreams started, they suddenly stopped. However, more and more, I began to accept that there is so much more to life than what lies right in front of us. I truly believe that, not fully see something, doesn't mean it's not there. I found comfort in this. I realised, more than ever, that we are never truly alone and I also grew to understand that we all meet again with our loved ones who have passed.

We all meet again. I have no doubt about that. This understanding has helped me to begin to come to terms with the loss of Lisa and, while it hasn't taken away the human suffering, I have found peace.

That first year after Lisa's death was certainly the most challenging in all my life. I dyed my hair dark like Lisa's, wore Lisa's favourite body spray which was sadly called 'True Love' by Impulse, and I suppose I tried to become more like Lisa in order to feel closer to her. I didn't really gain much comfort from this and, in time, I understood I was not helping myself. It was important to love all of my beautiful memories of Lisa and to remain myself.

This became clear to me, one night, in a very vivid dream.

During the dream, I opened my bedroom door and saw Lisa sitting on the bed, smiling.

"Angela," she said, in a calm voice, "you have to let me go, you can't keep holding onto everything."

I started to cry. I felt devastated, telling Lisa that I could never ever let her go.

"How can you ask me?" I demanded.

She told me not to let go of our lovely memories but to let go of the pain and suffering, that it wasn't helping me.

"You need to mind yourself more," Lisa told me.

When I woke up, I knew that Lisa was right and I knew I had to start letting go as much as I could. At the same time, I also knew I was a woman whose sister had been murdered and people couldn't expect me to let go completely.

Random strangers would approach me and hug me, which was nice and also strange. My photo was in the paper that I work for so people knew what I looked like and were aware of my loss. I had people tell me that they would not be able to cope with what I was going through. I could see the fear on their faces. By talking to me and meeting me, they felt that anything could happen to a member of their own family at any time. I couldn't provide them with the answers they needed at the time but, hopefully, Lisa's story can help.

Sometimes, it would be the little things, not the big things, which were most difficult to deal with. At one family gathering in Leighlinbridge we were told by a relative, for some inexplicable reason, that on a map of Leighlinbridge it shows a back lane leading up to the house Lisa rented. We were told it is called Murdering Lane and that it had always been called that. None of us could believe that a lane could actually be named that. Hearing this left us feeling uneasy and disturbed. The lane led to the back garden of the house Lisa lived in. Those things catch you off guard. Equally, there are things in life which will pull you in and protect you.

Between work, counselling and getting through my fears and phobias, our first summer without Lisa had almost passed. I took a week's holiday to Lanzarote with Steve. It was nice and quiet and, while part of me relaxed, being far away from the rest of my family made me feel more insecure and vulnerable. I suppose, I worried more about the rest of them. I was dreading the thoughts of the court case yet part of me just couldn't wait to have it over. We all wanted answers, even though we knew that no answer we received could ever help us. I suppose we needed to know the full story so that we could begin to heal.

However, before the court case, we had Lisa's one-year anniversary to get through and, just a few days before that date in September, we learned O'Hara had pleaded guilty to the charge of murder.

The news came on a Friday evening. I'd been feeling really tetchy and emotional that day, especially with Lisa's anniversary coming up, and the call couldn't have come at a better time. It was Jane who rang me, telling me that he had pleaded guilty and that he could never back out of that plea. Instantly, I felt like a weight had been lifted off me.

This meant that there would be no need for a jury and there was a chance we'd spend only a few hours in court. Importantly, it also meant that we'd spend less time in the same room as him. I cried from the relief and wondered what had made him plead.

Shortly afterwards, one person too many said the wrong thing to members of our family upon hearing the news. One person said, "In fairness to him ..."

That phrase made my stomach turn.

His guilty plea was not for our benefit. I know that. As for people's choice of words, I was quick to correct those who used phrases like, 'In fairness'. I was quick to remind them that there was nothing fair in it. However, I will admit that I thanked God that the case was not going to go to trial. I'm not sure what way I would have come through it, how any of us would have endured such an event.

I didn't realise how pent up I had been for so long, until the tears and breath escaped me after hearing about his guilty plea. I had no idea how wound up I had been until that moment. It meant we would have Lisa's anniversary and, shortly after that, perhaps, we might also have some closure. We might be able to start healing.

Lisa's Mass was held on the following Saturday evening in the church in Bagenalstown.

CHAPTER 12

It was hard to believe that a year had gone by since Lisa's murder.

We all had that haunted look in our eyes and, even if you didn't know our family or our story, you would have been able to tell that something very sad lurked behind our forced smiles.

The Saturday we held the anniversary Mass for Lisa we all looked wounded. One of my good friends had flown home that morning from Corsica to be there with me and, even though it was great to see her, I was extremely anxious and not at all good company. I could not control the emotion that had taken over that day. I was jumpy and wound up. If anyone said anything to me I was capable of flipping at them.

It wasn't necessarily because of Lisa's one year anniversary Mass, it was the fact that it had been a full year since I had spoken to my little sister.

It hit me like a tonne of bricks that 12 months had gone by, and it struck me hard. I found myself locked in my bathroom crying hysterically at the pain of our loss. No matter how many people advise you to take it easy, to take it one day at a time, you still find it hard to accept that your loss is permanent. You can't just wipe someone out in that time as if they never existed. You can't forget all those chats and lovely laughs you had together. As the weeks and months go by without them, you really feel it. It is the most impossible feeling, to think that someone so close and beloved is no longer there.

I knew that I wasn't alone in this. We were all feeling the exact same but, if I could have, I would have wanted to feel that way alone. It's not easy knowing that the rest of your family is suffering, too, it only adds to your own sadness.

Lisa's anniversary Mass was arranged for 7pm in the church in Bagenalstown. I got ready in my apartment in Kilkenny and planned to go out afterwards in Kilkenny, anything other than sit at home in my apartment wallowing in misery.

When we got to St Andrew's Church it was packed, there were so many relatives and friends there to remember Lisa. Unlike the funeral, this time I could actually talk to people. I stayed at the back of the church, in my own little corner, listening to the sermon and the beautiful Bagenalstown choir that sang on the night. When Mass ended we all made our way out for a drink together as a family and we spoke, briefly, about the upcoming court date which was now only a few weeks away. We hadn't seen each other since we had heard the plea. We had only spoken over the phone so now we could talk some more about it.

We all agreed we were dreading it but, at the same time, we were glad we had the plea and the earlier court date, so that soon it would be one chapter closed in this horrendous nightmare.

We hadn't told anyone other than our partners and close cousins about the plea or that the court date had been brought forward. When people had first heard the trial date many said they would come up to Dublin to be there for us. While that support was appreciated, what we really needed were a few close people with us, not a massive gathering. We knew, instinctively, that that was how it should be. So, we said nothing about the new date and instead concentrated on preparing ourselves for what lay ahead.

That evening in Kilkenny, we tried to feel normal and chatted to the friends and relatives who had joined us after the Mass. As I looked around, I could see that most people had looks of pity on their faces for us.

I'm not good with people pitying me but I had to learn to cope with it. I've always tried to remain strong and positive in my life but, of course, this wasn't going to be one of those situations. It was too heart-breaking and there was no denying our suffering.

We didn't stay long in Bagenalstown and about an hour later we said our goodbyes and headed to our own homes. I went out that night in Kilkenny. I don't remember much about it. I had two drinks. I only knew I didn't want to be out and I didn't want to be at home. I didn't want to be anywhere.

We had been told a few days before the Mass that the detective in charge of the case wanted to meet us in Carlow that Sunday, the day after Lisa's anniversary. It was to be brief and he was to give us an overview of what to expect ahead of the court date. In a way, we thought it wasn't the right weekend but, on the other hand, he was the person who could give us an insight into the case and a better idea of what to expect on the day. We were all under the impression that the meeting would take an hour or so in the Garda station and, naively I suppose, that it wouldn't be tough. We thought we'd be receiving information in a straightforward manner.

When I got home from Kilkenny, I lay in bed just thinking of the year we'd had and what was to come in the following days and weeks. My mind was working overtime. Sleep escaped me. I kept hearing Lisa's loud, infectious laugh over and over. I could feel her hugs that were always so warm and comforting. I could see the lovely smile that lit up her whole face. I was seeing her as a child, so generous and kind, and as an adult, so beautiful and endearing.

I could see all I had lost and gained all in the same moment, and I wrapped myself in my own arms, pretending that, when I closed my eyes, it was Lisa with me, holding me, reassuring me, telling me that everything would be okay.

But, of course, I had to get through the next few weeks. Then, maybe, I would feel normal and strong again. I refused to be beaten in those darkest hours and, whatever the meeting with the detective would hold, I would be ready.

I promised myself.

CHAPTER 13

After no sleep and a very emotional night, I got up, showered, ate a small breakfast and prepared myself for the day ahead. As it was only siblings allowed into the Garda station to meet the detective, I told Steve it would take no more than an hour and I'd call him afterwards so that we could spend the rest of that Sunday just relaxing and taking it easy.

How wrong I was.

I texted the rest of the family and we arranged to meet at midday, in the car park in Carlow town, just across from the Garda station. We weren't prepared for what lay ahead. Looking back, I know we had absolutely no idea what was to come.

We walked into the station and asked for Detective Murphy.

Two minutes later he came out to greet us and I remember thinking how pleasant he was. We first made our way to one of the rooms but someone was already in there, being questioned. Sickeningly, the only room that was free was the very one that Ger

O'Hara had been taken to only 12 months before.

It was a small room and the detective went to get more chairs for us to sit on, it was very unsettling and strange. We weren't sure what way to feel about any of it.

The detective then spoke about the court date that lay ahead. As a result of O'Hara's guilty plea, the case was due for court on October 5, a week earlier than the original date. As he had pleaded guilty, we were informed that not everything would be presented in court – such as witness statements and other statements given by people – as these were now no longer needed. It was very clear that the Gardai and Detective Murphy had covered all areas and a lot of people had been interviewed. It was clear that no stone had been left unturned.

Most people don't realise the amount of work that is done behind the scenes and we didn't until that moment. We were certainly more appreciative of the Gardai and those who worked on the case afterwards. Detective Murphy had not been at the station in the early hours of the morning of September 20, 2009. But he later arrived to question O'Hara.

He told us O'Hara had arrived clutching a letter and pulling at his hair, screaming, "I've done a terrible thing to Lisa." He then presented a letter to the female garda on duty who thought, at first, the letter was a suicide note. It was written with the address of the house in Leighlinbridge on the top right-hand corner, almost like it was being written to send to someone. It had his name written at the end – his signature, followed by three kisses. I felt that I was going to vomit as we were handed the letter. His handwriting wasn't messy. It looked very neat. He admitted in the letter he'd had 'urges' to hurt people from time to time, especially when he had been drinking. He also admitted he knew, one day, that he would do something bad.

He spoke of how he had loved Lisa more than anything in this world. How she deserved better. How he never wanted forgiveness for what he had done. How Lisa was such a gentle person and was in no way to blame for what he had done. He didn't know why he had hurt Lisa. He was sorry for everything.

Detective Murphy had asked O'Hara what had happened.

O'Hara said he could not explain why he had murdered Lisa, but admitted that he got the urge to strangle once or twice a year. The letter went on to say that he could never explain what he had done, because he did not know why.

O'Hara wrote that, when he drank alcohol, he had terrible thoughts, adding that he loved Lisa with all his heart and that she deserved better. He said that he'd never meant to hurt Lisa. But when he was asked if, at any point, he had attempted to resuscitate Lisa, or try to save her life, he just told them that he did not know any first aid.

I was so angry.

Of course he knew first aid, even children know the basics of first aid, and someone playing sports knows the basics of how to breathe life back into someone. I had learned how to do CPR at 12 years of age. But, of course, O'Hara was never going to try that. He wanted Lisa gone and he was making sure she was never coming back.

Having received this information the Gardai visited the house in Leighlinbridge. They found Lisa's body lying under a duvet in their upstairs bedroom.

In the interview, O'Hara had told gardai that he and Lisa had spent the Saturday night socialising with Lisa's sister and her partner. Detective Murphy told us that, from the statements given by people who were there that night, O'Hara and Lisa appeared to be in high spirits. The CCTV footage revealed the two of them were holding hands as they walked to a local pub over the bridge in Leighlin.

We needed to know more. The hours started to pass by as we remained huddled in the small room. The more information which was revealed to us, the quieter we became. I started to feel numb.

My head was spinning and everything around me seemed to be fading out of sight.

O'Hara had been cold and detached when he was talking to the Gardai. Gone were the hysterics he had produced upon his arrival at the station. And, when O'Hara's mother was called to the station, he laid his head on her shoulder and sat there, saying nothing.

We found out that when O'Hara was brought to Castlecomer court that Sunday afternoon, he had been given the option of covering his face on his way into the court to avoid the cameras, but he had refused.

We spent over three hours in the Garda station being prepared for the court case. We were told that the hearing would last a few hours and that we would be in court for only one day. We were also given the option of seeing the court room before the date.

It was after 3pm when we left the station. We had all missed phone calls and texts from our own families, who were worried about us.

I called Steve, but was barely able to get the words out. He had been sick with worry, as he had no idea how I was going to take the news from the detective and he'd become concerned when I wasn't answering my phone. I told him I'd be home soon, that none of us had realised the time and that we hadn't even broken for a coffee break.

We stood outside the station for some time, breathing in the air deeply, and trying to recover from the shock. Most of us were crying. They were silent tears. In our minds, we now had the brutal, horrifying images of what had occurred in the early hours of that morning in Lisa's home. We all hugged. We said our goodbyes.

We were tired and traumatised.

I don't remember the drive home to Kilkenny but when I got into my apartment I couldn't speak. Any conversation, whatsoever, was beyond me. I ate whatever Steve put in front of me and I sat there for over an hour, saying nothing. As hard as I tried in that time, I could not physically get any words out.

I was still numb and in turmoil.

Eventually, I asked Steve if he wanted to go for a walk. I needed to get out in the air and try to clear my head. It was a sunny day. Walking was good and I slowly found myself recounting what we had learned about that moring when O'Hara had gone to the Gardai. I told Steve what O'Hara had said, about the letter, the urges he had spoken about, the evil of it all.

I burst into tears as I spoke. The more the words came out, the greater the sense of reality of what had happened. I thought the tears would never stop. I was so sad and kept wondering how I would ever sleep and feel right again after learning of how my little sister had died. We had known the barest of details for over a year but, now, we knew everything. I felt drained. It had being such a tough morning. The whole family felt battered by it all.

Although I was exhausted, I didn't sleep that night. I couldn't close my eyes without seeing my little sister on the last night of her life. I kept thinking how much better it would have been if I had not known the full facts. That way, I would never have had such awful pictures in my head of Lisa's final moments.

The following morning I went to work but I soon realised I couldn't stay there. My workmates didn't know what I had been through the day before but I spoke to my editor and explained what had happened over the previous 24 hours. She remarked on how ill I was looking and understood that I needed to go home.

I went home and spent the entire day in tears, working through the emotions. I couldn't wait until Steve got home from work so that I wouldn't feel so alone. That week was one of the toughest weeks of all.

It had been a painful experience but, now, we all knew what to expect when we walked into the court room. None of us was under any illusion. It was going to be overwhelming and excruciating. Detective Murphy had asked us if we still wanted to do a victim impact statement, informing us that it was within our rights, regardless of the plea.

I knew I wanted to write something and, this time, I knew I'd be able to get up on my feet and read it out. I wasn't going to be using any Valium or numbing medication to get through it, those days were gone. I was never going to go back to that period in my life again. I was going to do this for Lisa.

I wanted to be her voice.

In the statement, I wanted to write about how much the loss of Lisa meant to us all. We had been told that statements are generally kept short, but there was so much I needed to say about her. I arranged to give it to Detective Murphy the following Sunday, so that he could read through it and pass it on to the legal people.

Writing the piece wasn't easy but it was therapeutic and it helped ease my mind after the horrible images which had taken up all of the space in my head. It allowed me to express the pain I was feeling. I felt sure that the one thing I needed to do most was stand up in court and read it out myself.

I spent the next few days coming to terms with what had really happened that night. I couldn't understand how someone could be so evil and do something so evil and senseless, and have the nerve to say they loved that person. But, I needed to leave him out of my life, there was no place for him there. Torturing myself over thoughts of him wasn't going to bring Lisa back, but it would bring me down and I couldn't let that happen.

O'Hara didn't deserve that power over me.

I prayed and prayed to have the strength to control my thoughts and, eventually, the searing images of O'Hara faded. I was ready for the day of the court case. However, I was worried about my father as he hadn't been with us the day the detective had helped prepare us. Though, looking back now, I'm glad he wasn't there. It took so much out of the rest of us and I knew he did not need to endure any more pain or suffering. Still, we felt we needed to prepare him in some way for the day that lay ahead in court.

Catherine called him in Donegal, where he had been staying, and ran through all of the essential details with him. I wish I could have been there to comfort him because I knew the further devastation he was going to experience.

My father is not a man for showing his emotions, or wearing his heart on his sleeve. He's a more private kind of man but I know that day he was broken, and heart-broken to the core. We did not believet that the court case offered us anything – we could not get justice, we could not get Li back.

All we could do was cherish our memories and try to embrace all the good times we shared with Lisa. I spent the next few weeks taking it very easy and trying not to stress over the smallest of things. I knew I needed to keep my energy up and be strong for the court case. I didn't go out and socialise. I kept to myself. I was no longer haunted by images and I was sleeping better but there was one more huge step.

We would soon have to sit in that court room and see Ger O'Hara's face for the first time since he had murered Lisa.

CHAPTER

In the days leading up to the court case, I could see Lisa everywhere. I was not having visions of her but I'd see someone in the distance and, for half a second, I'd imagine it was her. Maybe someone was wearing something she'd have worn, someone laughing like her, someone throwing their head back with the laughter and displaying that inspiring energy Lisa had. For that half a second, I'd get a little excited. You know that feeling you get, when you recognise someone? You're happy and surprised to see them, and you're instinctively rushing to greet them? I'm sure, in those few days, I got some funny looks from girls wondering why I looked so happy to see them.

This happened all through the week before to the court case. Time after time, it happened, and time after time I was surprised and excited to see or hear Lisa. Strangley, it was not all that upsetting. It was lovely and strange at the same time. I felt it was Lisa's way of letting me know she was never too far away.

Rita, my counsellor, also came to see me a few days before the case. We spent a few hours together and she prepared me for the court case the best way she could. That was my last session with Rita. It was my choice that we wouldn't meet again as I felt the rest of my journey was down to me. I couldn't thank her enough for all her kindness, she was truly a wonderful woman who was there just to listen and offer me any advice she could.

Rita reminded me not to go into the court looking for answers. There were no answers to be found, none that might bring peace at four in the morning when the walls feel like they're crushing in. She mapped out the court room for me and explained the detached nature of the setting. She also explained how emotionally fragile I would be afterwards and to go easy on myself.

My work with Rita taught me how important it is to avail of the help that's on offer and that a person who's trained in the area of homicide and grief can offer answers to difficult questions that we repeatedly ask ourselves. The Support After Homicide group is available free to families for two years after the event. I found it an amazing service.

I had been given one week compassionate leave from work the week of the court case, but I also decided to take another week of holiday time. I had learned over the year not to fool myself into thinking I could manage my pain in such a short space of time. Also, as someone working in the media, I knew that if I went back too soon after the court case I would be left with no escape at all, as the events would have been all around me.

While my own newspaper decided not to cover the court case, out of respect for me, there was still no opportunity for me to hide from all the other headlines and reporting, locally and nationally. Some sensationalised headlines are very difficult to accept. I wonder, when journalists are writing such headlines, do they ever even for a second consider what the families are going through?

I know they don't.

They don't think of a family member shopping for milk or bread in the morning and having headlines in the newspapers screaming into their faces. The hardest part for me was when my oldest nephews saw these headlines after Lisa's death. If what had happened wasn't already traumatic enough for them, they also had to be faced with that, and with the possibility of any child in the schoolyard repeating the story to them.

Most newspapers were very sensitive to us as a family, but not every newspaper. We knew it was something we had to live with, for a period in our lives, and that we would have to get through it and not get beaten up by things outside of our control. After all, Lisa had been taken from us. What could happen that was worse than that? We had all hit rock bottom, we had all gone to the darkest place ever. There was not much more to fear in our lives, surely?

However, when you've lost so much, you are faced with your own mortality and you are reminded, all too clearly, that nothing is forever. So, it's best to let the trivial things go and realise that only the big things, like family, and those closest to you, are what matter. I was no longer concerned with what others thought of me. I was only concerned about my own family and their thoughts, their opinions. That's all that counted.

The weekend before we went to court, Steve and I tried to relax and make an easy time of it. We still didn't go out and, instead, stayed at home watching movies and just relaxing and preparing for the dreaded day ahead.

Steve had booked a day off for the court case and had taken holiday time for the week after. I told him I'd be fine the week of the case and once it was over I'd just be sitting at home, taking it easy, recovering so the week after would be better as we could do something together, go somewhere, perhaps get away from it all.

I knew I had to get past that first week.

Once the case was done, I could take back control of my life. I wasn't looking forward to sitting in the same room as O'Hara and I didn't like the idea of the court room being so small and having to sit so close to him.

I didn't know how awful that would be until the day came.

The weekend before, I meditated. I spent a lot of time alone, just minding myself in preparation for what was to come. Those evenings I slept soundly. And, right up until the night before the hearing, there was nothing getting in the way of my sleep.

CHAPTER 15

The night before the court case Steve and I went to bed early. I didn't think too much about the following day and refused to let my mind race away. Instead, I convinced myself that tomorrow would be just another ordinary day.

I slept right up until my alarm went off.

I had my shower, got dressed, ate a small breakfast and then we made our way to my brother's house, as he was coming with us along with his partner, Margaret. Steve was driving. The journey was quiet; we were all just lost in our own private thoughts.

The family were coming from different directions so we all decided to meet at Houston Station as some of our relatives were getting the train to Dublin. It was also only a short distance to walk to the Central Criminal Court. We weren't due in the courthouse until 10.30am.

As we all met, there was a touch of anxiety in the air, as well as the knowledge that the toughest year of our lives might shortly be put to rest before we tried to rebuild our lives. All our partners were there, my two uncles, my mother's brother, Ned, and my father's brother, Michael. My closest cousins, Natalie, Lisa and Laura, were also there to support us. We had everyone we needed by our side as we walked up to the courthouse.

Outside, as we made our way up the steps, several photographers snapped away, not sure who we were but taking pictures just in case we turned out to be in some way newsworthy. Entering the building felt strange. The inside of the courthouse was massive and intimidating. I was full of nervous tension, squeezing Stephen by the hand.

"This was not meant to be my life," I said to him. "I can't believe this is part of my life, this was never how I pictured my journey."

God, I was angry.

I felt we had already been tested to the limit by losing Lisa and, now, to double our punishment we had to face this. Steve also felt overcome with distaste for every minute of what we were enduring. We made our way upstairs, but the courtroom was not yet open. Detective Garda Murphy came across to meet us and he made sure we were all okay. He wanted to check if I was still prepared to read out my statement in court. I told him I was.

He explained that the room would open shortly and that it would be best to get to our seats early, as the room would get very packed and we didn't want any members of our family or friends to be standing for hours.

We made our way into court.

We decided to take the second-last row, in the centre pew, and as far away as we could be from Ger O'Hara. But, in such a small room, far away was never going to be far enough.

No matter where we sat we were all in eye-shot of him, and he was of us. There was no escape. More and more people filtered through. There were a few cases up that day and the judge was going through the jury selection for them. The judge was asking people if they were available to sit on a jury for the following two weeks if necessary. When I heard that I felt so thankful that we didn't have to sit in the room for even a second day, never mind two full weeks.

As we waited, I wondered how families could possibly go through such hell on earth, sitting in that room day after day. I don't think I could have endured it, in fact I know I couldn't have. It's such a stifling place and it's emotionless and draining – my heart just goes out to those poor families who have to go through the long jury process. It takes an unreal strength to sit there and get through it and it's another reason why loved ones of muder victims need to treated so gently after a court case of this nature, because they are extremely fragile and almost broken.

I still didn't think, for one second, his guilty plea was to benefit us, certainly not. But in a way, it was one small mercy and I couldn't help but feel Lisa was protecting us the best way she could. There were so many witness statements and so much more evidence we would have had to sit through had it been a trial that I'm not sure any of us would have been able for it.

The heat in the room was making my head spin, I felt so sick that I had to desperately try not to vomit.

How am I going to walk up there, and read the statement without throwing up? I asked myself.

"I can't do this," I told Steve.

"I'm afraid … my legs … they won't carry me."

"Angela, you're the strongest person I know," Steve told me, looking directly in my face and being his amazingly brilliant and supportive self. "And you're able to do this. You're doing it for Lisa, remember. You're her voice … it's about Lisa.'

In that moment, I felt re-energised. I knew, when the time came, I could do it for Lisa. I could, and would, be able to stand up and speak to Ger O'Hara and everyone in the courtroom. When I looked around at my family and how pale and sick they all looked it started to sink in where we all were and who was going to be sitting across from us, soon.

Two hours passed before O'Hara was called up.

I kept looking over at where he would walk into the court. I wanted to be prepared for his entrance. I glanced over in that direction time and time again, but he didn't come. Then, the next time I looked, he was standing there. My stomach lurched. I could feel the vomit at the back of my throat burning me, and I felt the entire room close in around me. It took everything in me to gather as much air into my lungs and calm myself down.

There he was, just standing there. The man Lisa had trusted, the man she wanted to marry. The man she said she had felt safe with, the man she wanted a family with, a life with. Finally it was no longer surreal or just a bad dream, it hit home full and fast and there was no longer any denying it. As I looked at him his head was slightly bowed and his eyes were scanning the room. He didn't look worried or scared, not to me, anyway. He looked more interested in who was in the room.

I could see him continuing to look around to see who was there. Maybe I was wrong, maybe he was feeling remorse, but I couldn't see that. I didn't want to make eye contact with him at that moment so, instead, I looked around and put my hand on my father's arm and asked him if he was alright.

My father looked far from alright. He didn't answer me he just kept looking right through me, it was as if he couldn't focus, and he was doing his level best to stay seated where he was. I knew, in that moment, how any father felt. For my father, this was the hardest cross for him to bear.

As O'Hara had already pleaded guilty there was no need for a jury. Also, as it was lunchtime, the room had become a lot quieter, thankfully, and the heat was less oppressive. There weren't too many of us left in there. Detective Garda Murphy was called to the stand and he gave his statement, describing how O'Hara had walked into the station early that Sunday morning and admitted he had murdered Lisa.

The letter from O'Hara was read out, in which he first apologised to his own family. "This was not how I was reared..." he began. He went on to say he was sorry that he had, "Let the Doyle family down".

LET US DOWN?

LET ... US ... DOWN? How could anyone have written those words? I didn't feel any part of the letter was remorseful. It felt cold and detached and clinical.

I was asked to approach the bench.

I had to swear on the Bible, and speak on behalf of my family and Lisa. I walked right past Ger O'Hara. My statement made no mention of him either.

When I sat down on that bench, the effect was unlike anything I had ever experienced. I felt as though the life was being sucked out of me. I had my written statement in front of me but I knew what I wanted to say without needing to look at it, but, at the same time, my voice seemed to belong to someone else. As I was speaking, I had the sensation of being outside my body, listening to my own voice, as though I was seated elsewhere in the room.

When I finished my statement I walked back to my seat. None of my siblings had heard my impact statement before and, up until that point, we were all managing to keep control of our emotions. When my family heard me speak about Lisa they couldn't hold their tears back any longer.

When O'Hara was handed down the guilty sentence, there was no emotion, no feeling of elation, there was just the understanding amongst us all that we needed to get out of there.

His legal team approached me outside saying they were moved by my statement and asking if we wanted to speak to his family. We thanked them, but told them it was not the right time for us. It wasn't anything personal against his family, they didn't share any of his guilt, they didn't do anything to hurt us, but what were we supposed to say? We were trying to ease our own suffering and keep our own strength up and we really didn't have the energy, at that time, to help anyone else. There was nothing we could do to help anyone, there was nothing any of us could say. And there was nothing there for us.

Walking out the door of that courthouse felt freeing, just feeling the fresh air felt uplifting. Finally, I could breathe again.

We made our way down the street to a nearby hotel for lunch. I didn't eat anything, I couldn't, not that day or night, or for the following few days. My appetite had disappeared. But it was good to sit around the table together, on the one hand relieved that it was over, but also drained. The sheer weight of the previous 12 months had been exhausting. At around 5pm we all made our way back home.

That night I slept on and off, waking in the middle of the night from the nightmares that had become part of my life, reliving Lisa's last moments. The next morning, shortly after Steve left for work, I turned on my phone and then the calls and the texts, everything started to come through.

If only families were allowed to have a break. If only there were no calls, no texts, not the day after such a traumatic event. The messages informed me what was in all the papers and warned me that some headlines were upsetting.

Reporters called to my father's house and my sister's home in Leighlin. No one answered the door. They didn't want to talk.

In the end, my father had to escape to family in Donegal in order to get some privacy. Catherine went to Carlow to stay with her friend that day, to get away from it all. There was going to be no rest, no peace, not yet.

Journalists put their business cards through the letterbox at my father's home and at Catherine's, too. I told them both to pass the numbers on to me and that I would handle it.

When I briefly spoke to the reporters and gave them our family statement they were grateful, not pushy. They were happy that they could complete their story. Of course, everyone wanted a few words about him, about O'Hara.

I answered with a 'no comment'.

I knew that if I said anything about him at that time that I would probably fail to express exactly what needed to be said. Even then, I knew it was important to wait until later. Until I decided, perhaps, to write a book.

The only radion station I spoke to the morning after the hearing was KCLR. In the past, I had occasionally produced 'The Sue Nunn Show' and I liked Sue, I knew she would be sensitive. But the calls from others didn't stop, they came from every direction.

Steve rang and asked if I wanted him to come home because he was really upset for me, and wanted to be there to help me. I told him not to come, I told him it was fine and that he needed to work.

It was sunny that October.

The day after the hearing I felt my mind starting to break down. I couldn't sit inside the apartment. I could only sit outside, on the balcony. I couldn't physically eat anything. If I tried to put a piece of bread into my mouth I couldn't get it past my lips without wanting to throw up. I was a wreck.

Despite all the friends and loved ones who had made contact I felt very alone. I didn't know for sure what a nervous breakdown was, but I felt I was about to have one.

Inside my four walls, my mind would wander. Outside was better. Outside in the air and in the brightness, I had some control. I kept telling myself all would be okay, that this was just the mountain of stress from the past few days, from the past year.

You're a survivor. And you have control. Don't let yourself fall now. I kept repeating those words and, deep down, I knew I would survive.

I'm spiritual but I can't say I'm religious. I attend church for funerals and weddings, those kinds of occasions. However, after a couple of days, I was drawn to the church across the road. I locked up my apartment and walked to the church. I turned off my phone for the first time and, as soon as I entered, I felt a peacefulness. My mind was no longer going crazy. My hands stopped shaking and I was no longer frightened. I sat down at the back. It was dark and cool in there but I felt light, I felt at home. There was no one else in the church and I didn't pray, I just sat there.

When I left and switched on my phone I saw that I had stayed for two hours. I had two hours of peace and tranquillity. I hadn't missed any texts or calls, nothing, and I was feeling almost normal again. I was also getting hungry.

As a vegan I would normally eat very healthily but, that day, I didn't care. I ate so much junk food – no meat but a lot of rich and unhealthy snacks – and it felt great.

I still wasn't fully myself and I couldn't wait for Steve to have time off work so we could get away, but I was making my way back to recovery. I knew for sure my darkest days were behind me.

I wasn't stupid enough to think it was all behind me but I was optimistic that there would be happiness ahead, too. There would be peace. I could, once again, look at the future in a more positive frame of mind. There might be more pain to come but, if so, I was ready for it.

I was prepared.

CHAPTER 16

Steve and I booked a cheap holiday to Tunisia thinking it would be good to get away and recharge. However, when the time came, just one week after the court case, I felt worn out and could barely get on the plane. I just wanted to stay put in my apartment and sleep. I was anxious about leaving my family for a week so soon after that traumatic day in court.

For the first few days in Tunisia, the emails and calls from reporters didn't stop. I couldn't relax as I was still too contorted with the pain of loss and would ring home to speak to my family all the time. I didn't want to sit in the sunshine and enjoy the moment.

As the week wore on, I began to loosen up and Steve did his best by booking little excursions and activities that would take my mind off everything. After a while it worked and we met a lovely English family at the resort who became our friends for the rest of the week. Their kindness and their fun personalities made me smile and laugh so that, by the end of the week, I was no longer as battered and worn out. I felt myself starting to lighten up.

Getting back home and back into my work routine suited me. It was nice to leave the past behind as much as I could and I tried hard to concentrate on the present. I was still fighting the anger within me and the remainder of October was a challenge as I found myself being irritable with everyone: Steve, my family, and nearly everyone close to me. I felt jealous of people not having to deal with my pain or walk in my shoes.

By the time November came around I was still feeling very alone. On November 10, though, there was a major turning point in my life.

At 10am I got a text from Steve wishing me happy birthday. I had completely forgotten it was my birthday. I never forget my birthday but that was a sign of how my life had changed and I realised how sad that was. My workmates presented me with a gift and sang 'Happy Birthday', which cheered me up a little. However, that day was different.

I was so mad at God.

In work, despite people being lovely and despite having the weekend ahead planned with my friends, I could see no joy. It was a Wednesday and, as I finished work at 2pm, I couldn't contain myself any longer. I went into the bathroom and the pain, sadness and sheer loneliness literally brought me to my knees.

I stayed on my knees, in that small bathroom, crying my eyes out and railing at God. Asking Him, why was I so alone. Why was I being tested to the limit, and when would I ever feel complete or feel joy ever again?

Why did I have to go on? I felt mad that I had to. I knew I couldn't give up but all I could forsee was a very sad, empty existence. I must have been in the bathroom a while. When I came out and sat at my desk, one of my colleagues asked was I alright. I pretended I had been sick. I didn't want to admit that I had been crying as I honestly didn't want to go into it all over again.

She then asked was I pregnant.

Instantly, that brought a smile to my face, as I laughed back at her, "No way! That would be a miracle. I'm not pregnant." But she persisted with her questioning and I began to wonder, What if I am pregnant? My God, that would be a miracle ... what if?

But no, I said to myself, firmly, that will never happen. An hour later I finished work and made my way home. On the way, I stopped and thought again about the conversation. Why not get a pregnancy test ... just for the fun?

I bought one at the pharmacy and made my way home. As soon as I got in the door I took the test and then forgot all about it. A while later, I remembered and thought to myself, I'll have to take a look.

There it was, the faintest line possible. It seemed impossible that the test could be positive so I called Jane and asked her advice. Of course, she told me what I already knew, deep down, that it looked like I was pregnant. A short time later, Catherine rang. She had just been to see a very good psychic! The psychic had told Catherine that Mammy was asking for me and she also told her that there would be a birth in the family the following July.

"I wonder how that's connected to you, Angela?" asked Catherine, still oblivious to my news.

"You know Cat, it looks like I'm pregnant and, if my dates are right, then I would be due around July! That's if I am."

I sat there, alone, with the test in my hand and I thought, My God, I wasn't alone! I'm not incomplete ... you've sent me joy, you've sent me a reason to smile!

I felt the light, and life, go through me and all of a sudden I felt whole again. I felt all the pain, all the sadness of the last long period of my life, leave me. There was a life inside me, reminding me I'll never be alone again. I had been sent a saviour, someone to rescue me, not from others but from my destructive self.

I could no longer party hard, I could no longer over-stress. Now I had a responsibility, a life inside that needed me to be at my best and healthiest. And happiest. That evening, before Steve came home, I sat there in our apartment and I was no longer nervous about the future. I could see a future. That was my turning point.

Of course, Steve came home and he started giving me all my birthday gifts. When he was finished, I said to him, "I have one for you, too."

Steve looked at me. I handed him the test and told him we were going to have a baby. He was a little shocked at first as we hadn't planned for it – we'd both decided to wait until after our wedding – but his shock soon turned to joy. We held each other in an excited long embrace, thinking of all the new possibilities.

As I grew bigger with the pregnancy, so too did my happiness. Each little flutter, every little kick from inside was a constant reminder that everything would be alright in our lives. I worried, of course, as I had been hit so hard in the previous year of my life. There were times that I was convinced that I'd lose my baby, but, as the months moved ahead, my confidence grew.

I was ready to be a mother. I could feel my own mother's, and Lisa's, presence throughout the pregnancy and I dreamt of them a lot. In my dreams they both repeatedly told me that everything would be good, and not to worry.

Our lives were about to be turned upside down but this time with happiness. There were those moments that I thought, God, wouldn't Lisa just love this. I could imagine her being so happy, wanting to be part of my pregnancy. Her excitement would probably have been greater than anyone else's as she was always so open with her enthusiasm and love. I wanted my baby to know everything about Lisa. I was determined to let him know all about his wonderful auntie and, every single week, I told the little baby inside me different stories about Lisa and me growing up together, what she was like as a person, and how much I loved her.

CHAPTER 17

Christmas came a few weeks after I discovered I was pregnant and it was a really special time. I couldn't keep the smile off my face.

Steve and I decided to go for an early scan just to see what was really going on. There it was, on the monitor, the smallest little bit of life kicking away within me. I have never known a joy like it. We were both so ecstatic and, even though we had a deep and strong relationship, especially after everything we had experienced together, this time it was the real making of who we were as a couple. My life had turned a complete 360 degrees, and I felt so blessed.

Lisa was never far from my thoughts but now I could whisper her name with a smile on my face, and chat to her with happiness in my heart. I could almost see her smiling, too, as if to say, Now I can look at you and be happy that you're happy. Ever since those early days of the pregnancy, I picture Lisa that way, looking back at me, smiling and happy that I am getting on with my life, laughing at the silly things that I still do, but knowing that my tears and sorrow were now under my control.

I still feel a pang of sorrow when I realise that Lisa is gone but it doesn't last very long any more. I know where I am with Lisa now.

Lisa definitely showed me that life is fragile, that you only have this one life. You must embrace all you have around you. None of us know what's around the corner and, instead of feeling sadness for the past, and anxiety about the future, be grateful for the now.

I was becoming free from my worries about the future and I was excited and thankful for my life. No longer did I wish to walk in anyone else's shoes, I was content in my own. If I could, would I rewrite our lives? In a heartbeat. And I'd bring my little sister back to me and to our family, where she belongs. But that's not going to happen. So, no, I wouldn't change my life, not now, not ever, because by doing that I would change having Lisa in it. Lisa was our gift, our Godsend, and how lucky were we.

I never wanted to put my life on hold, spending my days at her graveside and screaming Why? I know that would have devastated Lisa, and I would not have gained anything from it.

The best thing to do to honour Lisa's life was to live my life. There was no way she would have wanted us to spend the rest of ours devastated, and hopeless. She would want only the best for us and to see us happy.

I loved being pregnant. I even welcomed the constant nausea as, to me, it was all for my baby. I felt a calmness like no other, and I was spoilt every day by Steve.

But another incredible discovery was about to impact our lives. I was about five months into my pregnancy when I received a phone call from my cousin, Laura, telling me that there was a woman trying to trace my mother. The woman's name was Susan. Laura had been contacted by Susan through facebook as her surname is the same as my mother's maiden name. As a result of that phone call my life and the lives of my siblings were about to change in the most positive and uplifting way.

Susan had being searching for our mother for almost 20 years.

Thirty-eight years earlier, my mother, due to circumstances and the times she was living in had no option but to take the heartbreaking decision to put her first child up for adoption. The story is my mother's and not mine to tell but I understand that she really didn't have any choice.

Now, after almost 20 years of searching, my mother's first child (my new sister!) had found us. It was amazing. Susan was so like us all, but she especially bore an uncanny resemblance to Lisa. Soon, we would also discover that her laugh and her infectious mannerisms were like Lisa's. Looking at Susan and chatting to her, we could almost see what Lisa would have been like in 14 years' time. However, Susan is her own person and she is not in our lives to seek to replace Lisa or anything like that. We had a new, loving member of our family. It was almost like God held out for those years for Susan and the rest of us, until the time was just right to bring us all together.

Susan's presence in our lives brought such healing. We all formed a very quick bond and it was almost as if we had never been apart. We chatted for hours on the phone and we arranged to meet a few months after our contact.

When the time came to meet, Susan came to Ireland for one week with her own family. Meeting her in person for the first time didn't feel awkward, not at all. It just felt right and was very easy and natural.

Susan's presence in our midst was joyous and it brought all of our family together and also helped us to reunite with our own extended family. This wonderful woman brought such happiness into so many lives. I could see Mammy and Lisa looking down upon us, and thinking how wonderful it all was. Life is very strange at times and can offer us ways and means of healing that we could never see coming.

At times, it feels like so much has been mapped out for us but, personally , I still like to believe in the mystery of it all. Susan's visit reaffirmed what a close bond we had as a family, and one we had almost lost through the weight and destructive nature of our grief. Now, we were all back, stronger than ever and we had another sister to share it with.

Susan is very beautiful inside and out, very like Lisa, and shares the same enthusiasm and laughter for life that Lisa had. We all feel very lucky and blessed to have her in our lives, reminding us that all is never lost.

I no longer had trouble getting up in the mornings, apart from when Steve would have to help me out of the bed when the baby bump took over! But life held only happiness and brilliant possibilities.

By July my due date was drawing closer and, not content to stay inside much longer, my beautiful baby boy came two weeks early. At 5.30am on Sunday, July 3, my waters broke. I stayed perfectly calm. At first I thought, *Crap! My bladder's now got a life of its own!* But then I realised what was really happening.

I thought I'd try to get more sleep rather than waking Steve up too soon so I closed my eyes, and there smiling at me were Mammy and Lisa, once more telling me, *It's going to be okay, Angela.* I closed my eyes tighter and went to sleep for another hour. In my dream I saw my baby boy, he was six pounds and five ounces, and I looked around the hospital room. I was in the theatre and I could even see the recovery room that I would go to afterwards. As soon as I woke up I decided to wake Steve, and tell him it was time. He was surprised at how calm and happy I was. As calm as anything, I told him I'd call the hospital in a while.

At 8am I was admitted to hospital. That Tuesday, 52 hours after my waters broke, my little boy eventually came into the world after a Caesarean section, weighing six pounds and 10 ounces – I was five ounces out. In every other way, my dream was accurate – the room was the same and even the recovery room was exactly like the one I had seen in my dream. So, when the midwife told me it was a baby boy I wasn't one bit surprised.

It was a blessing that the birth took the course that it did, though. After they induced me and told me that my contractions were very strong they said I ought to be in pain, but I wasn't. Despite having given me the highest dose of drip to induce the baby I still didn't dilate more than two centimetres in the first 12 hours. Baby Steve eventually emerged with the umbilical cord around his neck, if I hadn't been given a C Section things might have turned out very differently. Thankfully, he was a beautiful, strong, healthy boy and I am so in love with him.

I can safely say there is no love to match it. What is quite incredible is that I would never have thought it possible to go from agony to pure ecstacy in the space of two years.

The baby looks just like his amazing father – I'm a lucky woman to have my two Steves.

CHAPTER

One day after my birthday, and four months after baby Steve came into the world, I walked down the aisle, on November 11.

It was 11.11.2011. I'm promised that the date is a good omen.

My sisters, Jane and Catherine, and my sister-in-law, Therese, were my bridesmaids. I chose white and purple as my theme because purple was Lisa's colour. Lisa and Mammy were very much a central part of our day and we lit two candles to representing each of them.

My priest, Father Byrne, had become a good friend during the difficult times we had endured.

Susan and her husband, Daniel, had flown over for the wedding. Rosaleen came along too. Our family was as complete as it possibly could have been.

My father was a proud man walking me down the aisle and it was, without doubt, an exciting and joyous occasion for all of us. It was a day for our family to come together not to grieve, but, instead, to celebrate all of our futures.

The more I looked back over the events surrounding Lisa's death, the more I began to realise that it was easier to write down my feelings than burden others with what I was going through.

I never envisaged that what I was writing would see the light of day – either way, it didn't worry me. However, I felt it was important for me to let people in. To show others the impact that one person's actions can have on so many lives.

I wanted people to know my little sister. I wanted Lisa to be defined by her life and not by her death. I understood there was no escaping what had happened and I didn't want to deny that, but my intention behind writing has always been for Lisa to come to life through my words.

And, for people who never had the pleasure of knowing such a beautiful person, to somehow discover who Lisa was, and who she will always be.

Lisa's light will forever live on.

Lisa's smile and laughter will never die.

Lisa's spirit is evident very clearly in the way we have all coped and lived our lives since her death. Lisa is that whisper in the night, when you think you can no longer cope. Lisa is there saying that everything will be okay.

Lisa is within each person who is living their life in a kind and caring way.

Lisa was, and always will be, there.

Looking back at Lisa's life and her legacy, I understand what a wonderful mark she has left. With Lisa, what you saw was what you got. I can't say I was always that way and I don't think many people I know are so genuine. But there was never anything false behind Lisa's smile. When she listened to people's stories she wouldn't drift off, as so many of us do. Lisa would hang on every word.

Lisa had no enemies, no one she ever harmed, no one was ever hurt by her actions. There was only love and kindness from Lisa. That's Lisa's legacy.

Her life reminds us all that if we are open, honest, kind and genuine, then what a comfort that would be. After losing Lisa, I certainly questioned my own actions and wondered what kind of legacy I would leave behind.

I came to the conclusion that, had I died at such a time in my life, I wouldn't have been one hundred per cent proud. Don't get me wrong, I'm not a bad person – I'm actually told by many people that I'm good. However, there were a few relationships I needed to mend and, since Lisa's passing, I have tried to do this. I have learned that my energy can affect the people who are around me so it is important to be in a positive space, a positive energy field, and to be conscious, at all times, of my actions. Not to be fleeting with my feelings and interactions.

We only have one lifetime to make an impact. We may not touch the masses but even the effect we have on our family and group of friends and acquaintances should be positive.

Each one of us should make time to take a good look at our lives, we ought to ask ourselves, When the curtain falls, will I be happy that I was the best that I could be? Will I be happy for people to remember me as I was, for ever more?

I can say that, a few years ago, If I had been looking back at the reel of my life, I'm sure I would have cringed at many of my mistakes. But I can bet that when Lisa sat through hers, she smiled and laughed, and was proud at all her actions during her life.

That's a movie I'd be proud to sit through.

The great lesson I have learned is to live life as fully and honestly as I can, and not to leave any stone unturned. I know how people are affected by death. When a famous person passes away the impact it has on others is to remind them of their own mortality: if they can die, then so can I. It is usually a wake up call for us all.

If we accept death, then we can really live life. We don't need to be scared because, remember, the very fact that we exist is proof enough that more exists. How could there not be more out there?

I don't believe that when we pass away that's the end. I have experienced too many unusual and sometimes, yes, scary experiences, which have confirmed for me that we live on. And, when the day comes, we will all be reunited with our loved ones.

Epilogue

If there's one thing I've learnt from the last three years of my life, it's that no one else has the answers for you. You have to find them yourself.

For me, I feel we need to let people talk more about their grief. Don't be thinking people are self indulgent if, a year down the road, or three years, or ten, they're still dealing with the pain of loss. As a society, we need to be more open about loss, talk more about it so that it's not such a heavy weight, or a major millstone to deal with.

It will always be painful, but if we learn to accept death as part of life, then we will all get through our loss in a better and more humane way. None of us can escape losing someone, or answering that call when our own time has come. I have faced my own death through my own loss and I am a better, and happier, person for that.

There is no more fear, no more denial and that is very freeing.

Naturally, I will always feel the pain of losing a loved one. Who wouldn't? There will always be sadness and pain, but there will also be acceptance which allows the whole experience to be less traumatic.

I know I will die.

I know that I am not here forever. I know that, I'm not fooling myself any more, and I'm grateful to not have the fear of death hanging over me any more. This has allowed me to truly live. I have vowed, for Lisa, to live my life in the very best way possible, to do all I can to honour any gifts I've been bestowed, to love openly and honestly and to judge less and accept more.

Writing this story has been a real journey for me. I've dealt with so many demons. I've cried, pulled my hair out at times, but, at the end of it all, I've found unreal strength and great healing.

I wanted people to know my little sister.

I wanted Lisa to be defined by her life and not by her death. I understood there was no escaping what had happened, and I didn't want to deny that, but my intention behind my writing has always been for Lisa to come to life through my words.

For people who never had the pleasure of knowing such a beautiful person, my writing might somehow allow them to know Lisa. This was something he clearly never wanted to happen for Lisa.

So, this is my way of making sure it does happen.

I also wanted Lisa's story known so that, when the day comes for his release from prison, this book can be a reference for others, that they can understand what he was like.

Too many times people get out of prison and, years later, others have forgotten. The family don't, but most people do. My mission was, and will always be, to keep Lisa's memory alive, and to make sure that, upon his release date, people know who they're dealing with.

We, as a family, may one day pass him on the street, in one of the shops, a local pub, who ever knows?

It hardly seems right, does it?

There, across from one of us, as free as a bird, might be the person who murdered Lisa!

But, as I've said, that's for another day. We cannot lock Ger O'Hara away for any longer than the justice system dictates but, maybe, some other families down the road who suffer the brutal death of a loved one, can see that another evil killer is locked away for a long, long time.

Maybe there will be greater justice for other families.